THE APOCALYPSE OF JOHN

SUPERVISION OF THE WORK
This work has been edited by the following persons:
Ilias L. Katsiampas
Vana L. Katsiampas
Spiros G. Polizois
Lamprini Sp. Polizois
Anatoli Fitopoulou
Terry MacCallum

Cover: Mediterra Books
Production supervisor: Platon Malliagkas – mediterrabooks.com

ILIAS L. KATSIAMPAS
OMAKOIO OF TRIKALA, GREECE
METAPHYSICAL STUDIES IN YOGA & SHIATSU
21 KEFALLINIAS STREET, 42100 TRIKALA, GREECE
Tel. no.: 0030-24310-75505 or 0030-6974-580768,
Websites: http://www.omakoio.gr or https://omakoio.blogspot.com
E-mails: omakoio@omakoio.gr or omakoeio@gmail.com

OMAKOIO OF TRIKALA PUBLICATIONS
© ILIAS L. KATSIAMPAS
IOANNI'S APOCALYPSE
AS EXPLAINED BY GREEK MASTER NIKOLAOS MARGIORIS
FIRST BILINGUAL EDITION (IN GREEK AND IN ENGLISH)
FIRST EDITION, TRIKALA 1999, GREECE, ISBN: 960-85735-1-3

SECOND ENGLISH EDITION 2015
«The Apocalypse of John as Explained by Greek Master Nikolaos Margioris»
TRIKALA, GREECE

ISBN 978-960-85735-6-7

The translation of the work from Greek into English was undertaken by
Eleni Kalkani (Member of the Association of Greek Translators)

ILIAS L. KATSIAMPAS
ESOTERICISM FOR ALL – ESOTERIC THEOLOGY

THE APOCALYPSE OF JOHN
AS EXPLAINED BY THE GREEK MASTER
NIKOLAOS A. MARGIORIS

Under the supervision of and with extensive
analytical commentary
by his student Ilias L. Katsiampas

OMAKOIO OF TRIKALA, GREECE
SECOND ENGLISH EDITION

DEDICATION

The Omakoio of Trikala wishes to dedicate this book to the whole human race without exception, to every person on Earth who has truly sought to learn the causes of his existence so that he can, according to his evolution, benefit from those elements that will help him realize the deeper Meaning of life, the Immortality of the soul and the existence of a Divine Plan to which he will one day conform and will then attain the quickest and safest path to his Inner Self and, little by little, to the Progenitor of All, our Father and God. He will be released from the ignorance that surrounds him and keeps him chained and feeble as a direct consequence of his full dependence on matter, and he will side with the Spirit, the **Light**, the **Love** and the **Truth**.

Also, the director of the Omakoio of Trikala feels the need to dedicate this work to his father, **Lambros Katsiampas**, has recently departed from our world and who was of sound mind and boasted well-balanced intellectual functioning within the framework of a rich psychic world, which is Important and Indispensable for the normal, healthy spiritual development of every man on the Esoteric Path.

Η ΑΠΟΚΑΛΥΨΗ ΤΟΥ ΙΩΑΝΝΗ

ΕΞΗΓΗΜΕΝΗ ΑΠΟ ΤΟΝ ΔΑΣΚΑΛΟ
ΝΙΚΟΛΑΟ Α. ΜΑΡΓΙΩΡΗ

*Υπό την επιμέλεια και τους εκτενείς αναλυτικούς
σχολιασμούς του μαθητή του Ηλία Λ. Κατσιάμπα*

ই৯

IOANNI'S APOCALYPSE

EXPLAINED BY MASTER
NIKOLAOS A. MARGIORIS

*Under the attendance and the extensive analytical
commendations of his student Elias L. Katsiabas*

ই৯

ΕΚΔΟΣΕΙΣ ΟΜΑΚΟΕΙΟ ΤΡΙΚΑΛΩΝ
ΔΙΓΛΩΣΣΗ ΕΚΔΟΣΗ
(ΕΛΛΗΝΙΚΗ & ΑΓΓΛΙΚΗ)
ΤΡΙΚΑΛΑ 1999

OMAKOIO OF TRIKALA PUBLICATIONS
BILINGUAL EDITION (IN GREEK AND IN ENGLISH)
TRIKALA 1999

First Bilingual Edition (in Greek and in English).

THANKS

We also wish to publicly thank and congratulate Kallia and Andreas, the children of our Master Nikolaos A. Margioris, for their continuous and consistent contribution to the reproduction of the publications of the Master's more than 180 works which they are supervising with particular care and genuine interest.

We also thank all those who contributed in any way to the publication of the present work: the students of the Omakoios of Athens, of Lamia and of Trikala who ordered the book. **Spiros and Lambrini Polizois** (who offered and continue to offer their whole being to the Master's Work), who, together with **Vana Katsiampas**, not only oversaw the corrections of the present book but also made invaluable suggestions, and **Sofia Skoumis - Katsiampas** who undertook the task of typesetting, paginating and editing the book.

Finally, we wish to wholeheartedly thank our beloved Master **Nikolaos A. Margioris** for the preternatural Work that he generously, with ample Love, Freedom and Respect delivered to us and to all the world **(Esotericism for All)** and to assure him that in accordance with the direct order we received from him, we shall continue from the trenches we find ourselves in and according to our powers, to serve this Work and the Divine Purpose, for the promotion of the Good and Honest, of the High and Spiritual, of the Perfection that our Master represented and represents as a humble soldier of Jesus Christ, whose Orders he followed and served and which crown ALL his work without exception.

A WARM REQUEST

All those who wish to use some parts of this bilingual work (Greek and English) are kindly requested to contact the publishing house (Omakoio of Trikala) and its director, as well as to cite the publishing house, the title of the book and the author, Ilias Katsiampas, so that the readers can search for the work in order to be informed first-hand about the matters that concern them.

CONTENTS OF THE ENGLISH EDITION

CLARIFICATION FROM THE AUTHOR

The Book of Revelation as Explained by Master Niko-laos A. Margioris was first written around 1998 and was published in Greece in early 1999 in a bilingual (Greek - English) printed edition. It is derives from N. Margioris' oral teachings during the 1986-1987 time period.

Today, we present its second international English edition which was completed in 2015.

The writing and presentation of this work in 1999 was a result of the great need that had arisen for the development of a somewhat more inner, spiritual response to the multitude of projected and persistent scenarios of the world's and humanity's destruction and deluge which had been presented by many sides-groups-sects, and also by individuals, members of the clergy or laymen, both in Greece and on a global level. All of these scenarios proclaimed in an almost aggressive way, that regardless of what any simplistic, in the majority, arguments or more apparently serious efforts disclosed, the destruction of humanity was imminent and that it would definitely occur by the end of 1999, always based on various prophetic scenarios, especially the Book of Revelation.

Then, due to the failure of their predictions, they grew somewhat silent, but, recently, several of them have returned, harsher and more demanding, either in a negative way (Mayan prophecies, comets, natural disasters, sun-spots, reversal of the Earth's magnetic poles, etc.) or in a more positive way in the form of promises for the rapid spiritual evolution of humanity, which is going to occur thanks to the arrival of positive energies, or the assistance of aliens. (More on these subjects will be included in the next book we have planned with the title: *The Mystery of Death and The After-Life Path of the Soul.*)

That's why, since 1998, apart from recording the Modern Greek Mystic Nikolaos Margioris' views on the interpretation of the Book of Revelation, which disconnects all the doomsday scenarios from the reality encompassed within it, an attempt has also been made to include Margioris' more general views on the present times and the near and more distant future in this book.

This was accomplished with **the extensive annotative comments in the prologue and the epilogue,** as well as our views which we feel help clarify the whole matter and explain the times we live in, according to the beliefs of Experiential Esotericism as expressed through the work of Nikolaos Margioris.

A newer book, which is still a work in progress, titled *The Mystery of Death and the After-Life Path of the Soul,* deals primarily with all the issues that lack of space and time prevented us from covering in the present book, and additional profound and useful explanations are given.

Naturally, not all of Margioris' views are included in this book, which was written quickly in order to provide an initial but basic response — well-documented and different from the current ones—to this multitude of would-be disaster scenarios (or even excessive soteriology) that had become very popular in those days and that, nowadays, have once again become mainstream in different ways. It is also **a basic spiritual outline of our times**, which remains quite relevant, and, as we would like to believe, useful and informative about the **timeless trajectory of man's spiritual evolution** and the deeper spiritual messages contained in the Book of Revelation.

The interested reader will find inner—and spiritual—analytical continuity and complete in-depth instruction on Cosmogenic, Ontogenic and Eschatological issues in other writings of N. Margioris, such as: *Posthumous Life, Esoteric Philosophy, The Birth and Death of the Worlds and the Beings (matter-antimatter-hypermatter, universe-antiuniverse- hyperuniverse), Raja Yoga, Christocentric and Christocratic Mysticism, Karma - The Law of Retributive Justice, Mystical Teachings*, etc.

Sincerely,
The Author
Ilias Katsiampas
Student of N. Margioris for a decade
and representative of his philosophical
and practical work.

DISCLAIMER

Ilias Katsiampas, the author of this book, has attempted to convey some of the basic and important knowledge he gained from the long-lasting, personal relationship he had with his spiritual Teacher, Nikolaos Margioris, in order to properly inform anyone interested in the deeper meanings of Esoteric Metaphysics. This knowledge, derived from the true experiences of a few of his fellow men (Mystics), not only focuses on the interpretation of the Book of Revelation, but also concerns any similar 'prophetic' work, either alarmist, or overly favorable to extreme soteriological scenarios concerning humanity's near or distant future, always in accordance with the views of N. Margioris.

At the same time, the author wishes to highlight the important and decisive role of the relationship between Teacher and Student throughout the course of improvement and spiritual evolution, which is OVER and ABOVE any disaster scenario of any material-morphic (outer or inner) world or promissory soteriology.

Any teaching, especially in Metaphysics, requires close and regular contact between Master and Student in the daily practice (see our first book titled *From the Master's Mouth to the Student's Ear*. The title of this book is inspired by the second principle of **Niyama** in **Raja Yoga**, which in the modern age is construed-presented as *"the Study of Books that deal with human spirituality and salvation"*. In the past, with no such books at hand, the perpetual, intimate tutelage *"from the Master's Mouth to the Student's Ear"* existed, instead) so that the initiation may be reliable, constantly evolving, of high quality, substantial, vibrating and more effective. Any other relationship, just like the one described in this book, has a purely informative character for the potential growth and moral-spiritual evolution-completion of every person, especially for those who truly desire it and willingly follow it not only in the context of special training and disciplined application, but also in their daily life.

The author has made every effort to make his subject matter easily understood by the reader and bears no responsibility for any errors, inaccuracies, omissions, or inconsistences that might be included in this book due to it being freely translated from Greek into English.

He also assumes no responsibility for any misunderstanding, misinterpretation and side effect, because this book is not a personal life coach, but a descriptive-informative medium of information and the conveyance of the author's knowledge, which everyone is free to meditate - reflect upon, to judge, to accept or reject.

It is everyone's wholehearted wish that the readers find an interesting, enjoyable, and useful study-course in the **Esoteric Empirical Knowledge of the Mystics** contained in this book.

Greece, Trikala, 1-12-2014
Ilias L. Katsiampas

INTRODUCTION

The present book is the result of the preserved Genuine Oral Tradition concerning the Apocalypse of St. John that was conveyed by the Greek Christian Orthodox and Spiritual Master Nikolaos A. Margioris to his students and that was further elaborated upon and shaped to contain all the open and exhaustive dialogues and discussions we tirelessly had among us for a series of years. It also includes my own crystallized point of view regarding the content of the revelations, as well as those of my fellow students who were present as listeners and with whom we actively participated in nearly all his activities and teachings until his natural end, in May 6th, 1993.

During these traditions –apart from everything else– he conveyed to us with particular modesty, clarity and directness his own Christocentric and Christocratic Mystical Experiential Explanation - Point of View of all that John the Apostle presents to us, which agrees absolutely with all his other written work and particularly with those books that examine the Eschatological Issue in Unique and Unprecedented detail and analysis.

The Apocalypse of St. John, as it was delivered by Master N. Margioris, was subjected to the scholastic elaboration of his student, Ilias L. Katsiampas (director of the Omakoio of Trikala), who took the initiative to publish it and who undertook with responsibility, consistency and accuracy, to transcribe the **EXACT** preserved words of his Master on paper, without any variation, sewing together only some points of the analyzed matter, wherever such a need arose. At the same time, he attended to all his works without exception and he wrote the necessary analytical and explanatory prefaces, comments, causes and purposes of publication, clarifications, ascertainments and the biography of N. Margioris and so on, which must accompany it in order that the reasons for the existence and the utility of such a work can be understood.

During the reading of the present work, it is recommended that the given explanations are compared with the text of the Apocalypse in order that this abstruse matter maybe better understood.

Also, for those who wish to study the Apocalypse of St. John in depth and/or to generally delve into Eschatological matters, it is advisable that apart from this work that constitutes a first penetrating and substantial analytical explanation of the disputed points of the Apocalypse, they should read **Margiori's** *Apocalypse* (in combination with his other works) many times and carefully as it is presented in his popularized book under the title *The Birth and Death of the Worlds and of the Beings (Matter - Antimatter - Hypermatter, Universe - Antiuniverse - Hyperuniverse)*, in *Posthumous Life*, in his work *Esoteric Philosophy* that is a Branch of the Correspondence courses of the Esoteric Key, in his essay *The Creation of the Worlds*, as well as in many of his 189 works, with a more direct priority to the following: *Christocentric and Christocratic Mysticism, Mystical Teachings-Volumes A, B and C, Theurgy Teaches the Eternal Way of the Soul, Patapios, the Humble Philosopher and Saint from Egypt,*

*Occultism- Volumes A, B and C, Reincarnation, Karma-
the Law of Retributive Justice, Three-Dimensional and
Four-Dimensional World,* his monumental work *The
Two- Volume Metaphysical Encyclopaedia, The Desym-
bolism of Greek Mythology, Raja Yoga, Kriya Yoga, The
Eleusinian Mysteries, Pythagorean Arithmosophy,* etc.

Trikala, 22-9-1998
Ilias L. Katsiampas
(Omakoio of Trikala)

PREFACE

We are going through a period in which Knowledge, all knowledge can and must circulate FREELY and in ALL directions, to EVERY thinking and cogitative person (some with more and others with fewer concerns and spiritual sensitivities) who simply wishes to become informed about everything there is to know or who is burning to gain deep insight, directly or indirectly, into anything concerning him as a spiritual entity in this world and particularly about everything that has remained behind the scenes and in obscurity until now or that has been abused and vilified unjustly and without cause by some people who could not or who did not want to see anything beyond their nose and by others who were afraid they would lose their kingdom on Earth.

Within these limits, we considered it our obligation to bring to light the Apocalypse of John as explained by Nikolaos A. Margioris, the Christocentric and Christocratic Mystic (he wrote and independently published about 180 metaphysical works) and to distinguish it as a Spiritual Work that differs from the earthly and generally untrue prophetic fury that is expressed with fanaticism, dogmatism and egopathy (individual or collective) or any expediency that finds expression through every rational explanation confined within the limits of a conscious or more rarely of a subconscious sceptocracy, not allowing man to see the Spiritual Depth and the secret Splendor that exists on the edges of the superior functions of his hyperconscious (spiritual) Mind.

The views that will parade before the reader in the main part of the work concern an Unprecedented, Uncompromising and Integral Spiritual Explanation (brief and substantial) of the Most important points of The Apocalypse of John based on the Mystic Vision of Truth, converted and composed into common speech, as it was Revealed in all its Greatness, Depth and Extent to Nikolaos A. Margioris, the Greek-orthodox Master of the Spirit.

But before we begin the study of the additional clarifications and comments of Ilias L. Katsiampas, the student of the metaphysical writer Nikolaos A. Margioris, as well as the explanation of the more interesting Semiological parts of John's Apocalypse, we must first clarify certain basic meanings, about which there is intense misinformation and misuse, although they belong entirely to the historical, cultural, religious, philosophical and spiritual field of the Greek-orthodox Tradition, resulting in the fostering and the maintenance of the confusion, the obscurity, the hypocrisy and the denigration of some people and of certain old or modern philosophical trends.

For example, the words Mysticism and Initiate (Holy Initiate, Mystodote, Mystagogue, Godlike, God-seer, Father, Saint, etc.) that express the Apogee of the evolution of the human spirit and constitute an indispensable part of our philosophical, religious and spiritual life before and after Christianity are meanings contained in the ancient Greek texts, as well as in the Hymns, in the Kontakia, in the Magnificat, in the Chants, in the Patristic texts and so on, of the Greek-orthodox Tradition and we use them in order to give the required Validity and the Full Spiritual Recognition to certain of our Worthy fellow men who surpassed all human limits and restraints, without, however, losing this contact, yet no longer being dependent on it.

These people constituted and constitute the Worthy Children of God who managed either through the path of Philosophy or Religion or Gnosticism, or even through the interweaving of these paths, to activate the highest function of their Mind, the hyperintellectual (spiritual) function of their Mind, and to communicate with the One Truth.

If we wanted to encompass the meaning of Metaphysics or otherwise Esotericism (that is, Occultism and Mysticism) in one definition, we would say that it is the Inner Existence of Everything. The Internal Texture of all Creation.

Of course, by extension, it is the Free intellectual expression and formulation of the Perfect Hyperintellectual Mystical Experiences of the Greatest Beings of Creation that passed through our planet and left us their glorified hyper-philosophical and hyper-religious Works.

Absolutely nothing is exempt from the Inner Initial Cause that is contained in the High meaning of the term Metaphysics. EVERYTHING depends on, is preserved and catalyzed by this. Because behind Metaphysics, there is the Life-giving Breath, Prana, the Holy Ghost, the Substance of the Hypersubstance of the Father that holds, administers and directs all Expression (visible and invisible).

On the other hand, the much-vaunted and sorely-tried Religiousness is an inborn quality existing in ALL people, a basic trait of Divine origin with which we go through life.

That is, it is the inner pulse, the vibration, the motivational Life Force (esoteric energy) of every man that activates us in every direction and that we consume accordingly with worldly or hyperworldly, physical or metaphysical works, always according to the qualitative evolution of our soul.

When the exoteric tendency of the soul prevails and there is a close attachment to matter through the Mind (which is extremely usual for all of us) we are talking about an exoteric waste of our Esoteric Life Force (religiousness).

Moreover, its exoteric matter-centric or formalistic rendering easily reaches the point of exaggeration, dogmatism, fanaticism, intolerance and extremism; of body-worshipping and human-centric manifestations of "piety" that often create a division, a rivalry, even individual or collective conflicts and almost never promote esoteric evolution.

On the contrary, when its inner expression (philosophical or religious) exists, it always leads man to surpass the childish nonsense and imprudence that he manifests because of the autocracy of thought (this sterile horizontal course) or because of the emotional fluctuations (exaltations) or attachments he had created on the basis of earthly sentiments, and it crowns him with the Transcendental Experience, the Deep Esoteric Mystical Experience by which he becomes a vessel of Creation with which he is united and by which he derives his rights from the Divine Source, and which allows him to face his real identity, the psychospiritual one.

Only then does one remain untouched by the games and trappings of matter (maya), does one truly become Pious (that is Religious – a knower of God) and sheds abundant light on our world with his presence, becoming a spiritual example to emulate, since he has managed wholeheartedly to express and to dominate his feelings internally and outside of his being and certainly, to constitute a beneficial cell on our Earth, full of spirituality and continually radiating the Truth.

According to Esoteric Philosophy - Theology, beyond their material clothing-presence, every person, is a psychospiritual being connected internally with the Deity-Truth, the only difference being that they do not perceive and do not communicate with this perpetual, internal existence of theirs because they are dominated by their external, outward attachment, by their intellectual and not hyperintellectual or subconscious knowledge of things.

Therefore, as long as the soul is governed by matter (in any form) and by its greatest ally, the Mind (consciousness as well as subconsciousness), it remains captive within the firmly-closed grip of a material or etheric shell which it accepts for itself and which deprives it of the true-secret characteristics and hypervalues of the Spirit that it bears within it and on the basis of the Freedom of choice, it suffers the spiritual limitation and castration that makes it believe it is mortal and that it ends its existence with physical death...

From the ancient times till now, there are three the Basic Indisputable Paths that elevate man from Earth to the Sky, from the Earthly to the Hyperearthly, from the Human to the Hyperhuman, from the temporary and the perishable to the Permanent and the Eternal.

The first path is **Theoretical Mysticism. Gnani** and **Karma Yoga** mainly belong here. Through action-activity, man shapes the called-for experience floating around and the essential knowledge to surpass the perishable reality and touch upon the eternal inimitable truth.

The second path is **Religious Mysticism**, within which belong all the Religious Systems of Mysticism that are based on the spontaneous emotional arousal of man, on the worship and on the unshakable faith in and love for the Divine Ideal or the reincarnated God, as for example, the Silent **Christocentric and Christocratic Mysticism** of the Greek-orthodox Holy Mountain Monks and **Bhakti Yoga** of India.

And the third path is **Philosophical Mysticism.** Here we meet **Raja Yoga**, the high intellectual or scientific or psychological art-union that according to Alice Bailey (on the basis of Djwal Khul's dictations), Vivekananda as well as my Master Nikolaos A. Margioris, constitutes the best and most effective way of educating the 5th Root Race, to which we belong, for the activation of the third and highest function of the Mind, the hyperconscious.

And this is so because the Science of Raja Yoga is by far the most appropriate method to instruct the Mind of modern man, whose demands for a clear analytical understanding of the ascending psychophysiology of Yoga are uniquely feasible and attainable through the intellectual exercises that will allow one to experiment and verify.

These are the Three Greatest Paths of the Esoteric Ascent of our world (most Mystical Systems belong to them), on which every man can firmly, confidently and safely "rest", according to his idiosyncrasy and to the natural inclination he expresses. Everyone can quite freely follow (be instructed in) the one he feels suits him most and vibrates him most deeply.

In any case, particularly in our days, **Esotericism** or **Metaphysics (the Free Esoteric Education)** are the **Alpha** and the **Omega** of esoteric training for the individual who is truly interested in approaching their Inner Existence, because it helps raise man's vibrations, his moralization, the development of Love, the creation of the

PUZZLE of **Truth** within him and his orientation towards and positioning on the path to Perfection.

After all, Metaphysics and Religiousness go together, hand in hand, and one does not exist without the other, even if there is some separation of the paths by which the human spirit ascends to the Divine Spirit (Scientific - Philosophical - Religious). This is due to the need that emanates from the personal sense of each of us (our internally activated center) and to the natural inclination we express that allows for the presence of religiousness within us in a unique way (evident or not), which automatically also defines the path that suits us most.

Finally, we stress that the highest form of Religiousness leading to Theosis is the spontaneous one, that is the one that attracts us in the most physical, rapid and secure way to the Divine (that comes from within); that is, the Mystical Esoteric Attraction - Call - Love (Religious Mysticism). However, not all of us are ready or properly prepared to express it because it is a matter of evolution and experience for every spirit-soul.

Extremely few are those who have acended this esoteric inclination. The rest of us are creating the conditions; some with the help of the Church and Religion, while others -- especially nowadays and depending on the tendencies they express and because of the general faithlessness that reigns due to the dominance of rationality -- turn to some other mystical systems of inner development that give the greatest weight to the analytical formation of man's "logic" concerning spirituality and to the teaching of scientifically-driven spiritual exercises that aim for the satiety of the intellect and the opening to the hyperintellect which will render us worthy of the Gift of the Holy Spirit.

What's more, the state of being Devout is real, to a greater or lesser extent, only when individuals have a **PERSONAL spiritual course** and when they follow one or more of the Ladders of Divine Ascent, especially by the side of an Initiate. But as this is rare, a spiritual guide -- (cleric or layperson) or even an Instructor of Esotericism who is directly or indirectly connected with the pure Spiritual Work of an Initiate or of a Master of the Spirit -- usually undertakes this role.

Finally, the full sealing and recognition of the Religious person constitutes a fact **ONLY** when he approaches the Greatness of Enlightenment - Theosis, which should be the aim of Every person on Earth ("The Son of God became man so that we might become God", Athanasius the Great; *"By the Holy Spirit every soul is brightened..."* Saint Seraphim of Sarov; and *"... the assimilation to, and union with, God, as far as attainable, is deification,"* writes Saint Dionysius the Areopagite.

I. L. K.

REASON FOR PUBLISHING
THE APOCALYPSE OF ST. JOHN
AS EXPLAINED BY MASTER
NIKOLAOS A. MARGIORIS

Many are the reasons that induced us to publish the present concise and comprehensive explanation of the MOST BASIC points of St. John's Apocalypse by Nikolaos A. Margioris, the Greek Spiritual Master.

First of all, we should point out that The Apocalypse of John has been in the limelight for quite some time but unfortunately, - in our opinion - not as it should be, that is, as a deeply symbolic text with interlaying **ESOTERIC Truths on multiple levels** which need experienced Occultists - Mystics (Initiates) to decipher it. However, through multiple and repeated undertakings of non-mystics; that is, of our fellow men who function intellectually (and not hyperintellectually-spiritually), all of whom, according to their constitution, their scientific education or any other specialization, their convictions, their external historical coincidental evolutions, their needs or influences and the concentration they devote to it, get some answers that as a rule suit and vibrate in tune with their conscious functioning, more rarely with their subconscious and almost never with their hyperconscious functioning.

This means that the rendering of the Truth on their part is presented quite superficially - exoterically, tainted and falsified, particularly when attempts are made to associate it solely with earthly events.

However, the Whole (hyperconscious-Deity) cannot fit into the partial (conscious - subconscious), the Infinite cannot enter the past. Even the hyperconscious, which is the only organ of the human-mind that has the inalienable privileged right to exercise a supervisory role on Creation and to approach the Creator through the individualized spirit-soul existing within every person, cannot transfer all these esoteric experiences exactly as they are to our rationality, despite all the changes that convert them from hyperconscious to conscious so that they may be comprehensible to others (something which is **EXTREMELY RARE** and **UNIQUELY IMPORTANT**).

Although these superior Experiences are expressed with the relevant meanings and concepts, they do not cease to contain the expressed Timeless Truths of a grounded Conception of Transcendental Multidimensional Hyper-realities while at the same time, constituting the Unchangeable Principles, Knowledge and Details of the Manifestation of the Divine Reality and of its Laws which those who seek spiritual Identity-Actualization should align themselves with and embrace.

Therefore, within these limits, the rationalists (surpassing science, Plotinus), as well as the ritualistic religious people (on the one hand knowledge kills, on the other hand the spirit vivifies) of each time period, who come face-to-face with metaphysical writings and try to interpret them, unwittingly or, more rarely, knowingly serve the work of the Antithesis (misinformation). In this way, they reproduce an "impressive" misprint, a horizontal (exoteric-materialistic) and not a vertical (esoteric-spiritual) one, an imitation of no import, value or spiritual content, which is relatively stimulating and arouses the interest of uninformed people, who are bound to the matter-centric - conscious perception of things anyway, and it is exactly this that continues to be welcomed and reinforced.

The consequence of all this is that the eschatological scenarios of Humanity and the dominion of the counterbalancing Power (Satan) that are suggested by exoteric researchers are adopted with little resistance by our likeminded fellow humans who are also spiritually limited and directly dependent on their bodily and egoic existence and are led to the easy solution, to the struggle for the imposition of the outdated, unreal and childish physiocentric view, by high or low standing, competent or incompetent individuals in an attempt to preserve their physical bodies from the impending destructions and the supposed future predominance of the Wild Beast – Antichrist. (In fact, every strong bond and every material or egoistic passion that guides our life defines exactly this, the victory of the Antichrist as we see it still in our days, within and without us).

This dull and dark scenario that is projected to the fullest around us and that easily passes within us produces only danger and outrage. And this happens because it creates strong fanaticism, intolerance, and absoluteness in the face of relativity; it arouses the primitive instincts of the animal-man; it awakens the intense passions and all kinds of excessive egocentricities (individual, familial, collective, racial, religious, national etc.) and an individualism that separates people from each other on the basis of external appearance, qualities and beliefs, which are a result of karma.

In fact, however, we ALL have within us the same **Inseparable** psychical eternal Presence-Substance, the unchangeable spiritual part of the Creator that we are not allowed to "cut to pieces" for the sake of some external traits we bear from one incarnation to another or in the name of a blind, unproven, ungenerous and often narrow-minded, dogmatic assumption that we have been served about God (naturally we share the responsibility that emanates from the low anthropocentric criteria we have concerning spirituality) or even in the name of an important but insufficient (continually revised) and imperfect scientific "conception" of the Truth (though it is hyper-metaphysical nowadays) at a level of quantum Physics and Cosmology ("every intellectual success is a new mistake of the Mind that replaces the proven untruths of the past, with supposedly new, verified truths of our times, " N. Margioris).

We cannot and we must not continue to be content with dead bread but we must strive and struggle to dominate our low and **unevolved** self so as to prove worthy of the Living Bread that will descend from the heavens and that will establish the Light of Knowledge and Truth Within us.

For this reason, what is required are daily sacrifices, year-long struggles, spiritual exercises, a spiritual guide (cleric or layperson, a true Knower - tortured and if possible, Worthy of the Calling of the Holy Spirit), as well as physical and intellectual-spiritual preparation that passes through the Church but ends up in our Inner Church, in our esoteric church ("For behold, the Kingdom of God is within you," according to the Gospel of Luke,16:21;

"you did not know that you are the church of God and that the Spirit of God lives inside you: if someone spoils the church of God, God will destroy him, because the church of God is holy, and these churches are you", the First Epistle to the Corinthians by Paul the Apostle 3:16) which we must create-clean-activate with great care and attention if we wish to become true hosts of the Spirit. Otherwise, how else could all this be done - with words, with theory, with rigid dogmatic beliefs? They definitely play their part and are of value because they bring man to the point of Understanding and Deciding to make the Great Change to Re-baptize and Spiritually (hyperintellectually) Regenerate himself ("Except a man be born of water and *of* the Spirit, he cannot enter into the kingdom of God", according to the Gospel of John 3:5). But apart from that, you need action - work, responsible and stable guidance and above all, you need to apply all you learn to life - first, to the life within us and then to the other one, outside us ("because action surpasses theory", Gregorios the Theologian).

Therefore, anything that binds us to absolute and immovable positions not only contains risks but keeps us locked up in a peculiar prison and limits us, forbidding us to have OUR OWN understanding of the Truth gained from personal experience or on the basis of the inclination(s) we have (scientific -Raja Yoga-, philosophical -Gnani and Karma Yoga-, religious -Christocentric and Christocratic Mysticism or Bhakti Yoga).

Whether externally or Internally, this is the purpose of man's evolution - to gain personal understanding of ALL things (earthly and hyper-earthly) and to gradually prevail over them, according to one's spiritual quality, likened and perfected until one once again meets our Father and God.

Following the above analysis, I believe that it becomes clear why such metaphysical texts should be handled only by Great or the Greatest Beings with a certified **AU-TOGENOUS Personal-Spiritual body of Work**, who, without fanaticism and with respect for all, can look at the Esoteric Causes and enter the Depths of Ecstasy, of the Dimension and the Conception of the same or higher Experiences and using the modern word, can reproduce in our World, some parts or the whole of these extraordinary and extremely interesting matters or interpret - explain the existing transcendental texts that have been written by their fellow men in the past (all this is based on a special Authority that comes from the acknowledgement of their Gift from the Holy Spirit).

In summary, we could say that the dark and misty landscape that unfolds before us, partly as a cause of the many attempts to interpret The Apocalypse of John or by unfortunate matter-centric prophetic scenarios that may or may not be related to the Apocalypse and that have recently come to the surface, creates a revival of instinctive passions, of medieval conceptions and of peculiar forms of egoism, covering or hushing up the Healthy Voices and leading people on misguided paths, to divided camps and to unjustified conflicts that show a strengthening of the binding of man with the exoteric side of the Antithesis (matter) which is by nature Divisive. Because, instead of using it for his spiritual evolution, man uses it for the satisfaction of his passions and his atomocentric beliefs that ultimately lead him to the total submergence within it, to the descent and the loss.

So, man is restrained within the limits of rationalism

(ring-pass-not, not beyond the ring of thought), of the mist and of darkness (of the "light" of matter), around which he builds his whole life and deposits all his spiritual dynamism, as if he will never die and as if he will take all the material things with him and as if only this is the purpose and the meaning of Life ("man does not live on bread alone" and "what will it profit a man if he gains the whole world and forfeits his soul"?).

And this, as well as all the suffering that will befall him, is man's curse because every one of his deeds (in thought, word and action) in our dimension moves and changes the natural texture and order of the world around him; it creates the causes that will bear the respective results and it sets the Divine Laws (Karma, the Law of Retributive Justice) in motion. In order for these Laws to be fulfilled, they oblige the unfortunate soul to follow successive reincarnations and endless psychosomatic torments and pains. This is the internal and external payment of the soul for all the acts it has activated against nature and against its fellow men. Also, it is the necessary contact it must have with matter, from which it will get the required experiences from the opposing powers that flood it, until it "is saturated" and turns again toward its inner spirit.

Nobody is exempted from the actions of his past, even if for one moment, it appears that he has escaped from the exoteric justice or if, without being apparently to blame, he pays off the damage, which means that he settles his old debts or that the humble desire or the interest of his malicious fellow men oblige him to suffer this psychosomatic trial, which, however, is credited to the positive account of his Karma. But at the same time, after his self-cleansing, his washing off of all the harmful events he had created and his release from all of his old obligations, he finds himself at the Initial, Prior, Clean and Pure Pre-descent state, the Spiritual one.

However, it is because of these ties he has with matter and the Ignorance that possesses him about spiritual things that man is lured and repeats the same, unchanged low thoughts and actions, "tasting" for the umpteenth time every fruit of matter, imprisoned in the vice of rebirths and of the inexorably erring hardships that have no end and that constitute the payment of his unwise choices which are turned into a hell on earth and a tyranny for his spirit-soul.

That is why we need Enlightenment **(Esoteric Education)**, any healthy Esoteric Enlightenment by our properly trained fellow men and why, when an Initiate descends to our Dimension, ALL of us must turn to him for "his help and support", because it is he who will remove the Darkness that is suppressing us and devouring our "insides" and it is he who will restore our lost Spiritual Dignity and INDEPENDENCE.

It is the Initiates who use the Modern LIVING and Vibrating Word to Reestablish, Restore and Revive every Metaphysical Value, Ideal and Virtue to our inner soul and give the indispensable Immediate Release of the spirit-souls (theoretically and practically) from the torturing bounds of matter. But for this Release, this Esoteric path to be established within us it requires special and great year-long effort and even -depending on the case- the effort of many lives from every soul that will decide to initially Know the Truth, to identify with it and to begin to gradually remove the decorations of matter it was bound to until the day before.

But, are we ready to face these Divine Beings? Do we have the criteria to recognize them? Do we realize that they may be roaming around beside us, silently doing their work and leaving their deposits for the future generations that will be more conscious and will perhaps be able, more directly and collectively, to walk the Path of the Spirit?

Are we ready to offer them our little services (in reality, these services concern us and not them who have no need of them) so that their work may become known? Do we want to walk on the "paved" Path that they offer us, overcoming our material descent and any hesitation and distraction?

Do we feel ready to at least become correctly informed about Spirituality and to prepare ourselves, even rudimentarily, for It? But where shall we find the Pure Esoteric Knowledge? Who will inform us extensively about it? How shall we overcome any arising problems, theoretical and practical? How shall we work steadily and unwaveringly on the Path of the Divine Ascension? Who will provide us with the necessary details and clarifications that are required? Who will help us get up when we fall and who will lead us to the Path again when we have deviated? Who will raise our vibrations with his words and work and keep the Spiritual Goal within us Alive? Who will truly enlighten us spiritually? Who will take care of all these issues and the many more that are too numerous to mention even in passing? Who will play the part of our Spiritual Father? Who is worthy enough to stand by the side of a spiritual Father? What must we do to gain this privilege? What will govern our relationship with him?

That is why the Obligation and the Right to man's **Free Spiritual Enlightenment** is needed, and that is why we felt it necessary to publish a Purely Spiritual Work (whose central figure is **Jesus Christ**) of a modern **Paul the Apostle, Pythagoras,** or **Vivekananda**, of a fully enlightened being that combines within Him all the above esoteric personalities and the qualifications that govern them, of **an ascended Esotericist** (Occultist and Mystic, that is, an Initiate), of Master **Nikolaos A. Margioris** (15-12-1913 to 6-5-1993). You will find some extensive notes about his life and his work in the book by his student, Ilias Katsiampas, under the title *From the Master's Mouth to the Student's Ear*, as well as at the end of this work.

We do not seek to prove the self-evident facts that concern the Spiritual Grandeur of our Master, nor of course do we wish to convince people- especially in our matter-worshipping times - in a dogmatic or absolute manner of the existence of an Initiate who walked beside us. This would be a mistake on our part.

Simply, with all due respect and humility, we consider it desirable and necessary to submit our personal testimony and all the relevant proof (his vast written work and his indefatigable, autogenous teaching that reached the point of self-sacrifice throughout his life) that we believe converge catalytically to support the certainty of our conviction. This belief also derives from our direct apprenticeship with him as well as the close personal relationship and cooperation we had with him for many years.

But at the same time, we wish for the in-depth Study of his Works (not only by those with a predisposition or inclination for free spiritual learning, but also by any well-intentioned reader) and for everyone to form a Personal Point of View about them and about the writer.

Finally, we highlight Paul the Apostle's Blessed and Crystalline words:

"And my speech and my preaching were not in persuasive

words of wisdom, but in demonstration of the Spirit and of power", to the Corinthians 2:4, or "We talk the Wisdom of God and not the wisdom of this world, For the wisdom of this world is foolishness in God's sight." to the Corinthians 3:19, and still "For I would have you know, brethren, that the gospel which was preached by me is not according to man. For I neither received it from man, nor was I taught it, but I received it through a revelation of Jesus Christ...." to the Galatians, 1:11-12.

I. L. K.

PURPOSE OF THE WORK

The purposes for which we wished to present this edition are multiple. First, we wished to Inform and to Enlighten, as much as possible, anyone who is seeking a more substantial and profound Hyperintellectual Spiritual explanation of The Apocalypse of John. Secondly, we wish to bring to Light and to the common experience of everyone concerned the personal Apocalypse of Nikolaos A. Margioris, which subsumes unprecedented Visionary Mystical Conceptions and revelations of this Otherworldly Work in extensive detail and with rare Unity and Coherence that definitely deserves to be Thoroughly studied by every well-intentioned person, Seeker or Researcher, Scientist or Metaphysicist.

Also, another purpose is that through Knowledge and Comprehension of the Divine Laws that rule Creation and Man, we hope that passions and extreme expressions that constitute the primitive manifestations of those involved (plunged in matter) and not of the evolved soul (released from the material bounds) may be moderated and if possible, be minimized, because as Jesus Christ clearly states: "... my kingdom is not of this world..." in the Gospel of John 18:36. Also Paul, the Apostle to the Nations, in his letter to the Hebrews writes that "they were foreigners and temporary residents on earth" 11:13, and also that "the flesh is hostile to God" Romans 8:7 and that "...flesh and blood cannot inherit the kingdom of God..." to the Corinthians 15:50. These are clear and correctly taught transcendental answers in the Words of God and his representative, answers that do not allow for any dispute or any vexatious interpretation.

Thirdly, with this presentation as well as the in-depth study of the other works of Nikolaos A. Margioris, the Metaphysical Philosopher, Writer and Spiritual Master, we wish to show that when it comes to explaining the Deeply Symbolic Revelatory Divine Texts any scientific or religious approach based exclusively on the intellect and on rationalism is condemned to failure.

Even with the aid of the most active and unbridled imagination of all of humanity, it is not possible for the True Dimension, Width, Depth, High Meaning and Spiritual Content of these works to be conceived, because the Vibration of the Conception and of the Comprehension of these matters is much more rapid, higher and superior than the vibration of the intellectual functioning of almost ALL the people on Earth, regardless of the position and the part that they have been charged with.

Only if we manage to raise our vibrations, to become morally edified, to become as perfect as "our Father in heaven", that is, to function on a hyperintellectual level, will we taste the Divine Fruit and will we start communing with the Divine Mysteries. There is no OTHER WAY than THE PERSONAL TRANSCENDENCY of the limits that we ourselves have placed on ourselves.

Otherwise, only the purified beings, the Mystics of the earthly years (and yet, not even all of them, but those to whom this Permission-Authority is given) can convey to us (privately or publicly) using common language the

Revealing facts that are in progress within them, so that we too can turn toward the same direction and struggle to regain the acquired rights we had lost due to our fall and to our close ties with the matter that surrounds us (of our spiritual castration).

Only the Mystics constitute a Truly unrivalled and ir-replaceable OASIS of the Inexhaustible Source of Spiri-tual Water. By their side, man comprehends his true ori-gins and feels his smallness before the modified Revealed Truth and God, while within him all the necessary feel-ings of ascension are developed, as much on the part of Religious Exaltation - Elevation on the Ladder of John, of St. Nikodemus of the Holy Mountain, of Gregory Palamas and many other Great Fathers, as well as on the part of the Philosophical Ladder of Pythagoras, Plato, Ammo-nius Saccas and of other Great Initiates.

Respect, modesty, self-sacrifice and the avoidance of absolute and extreme beliefs that serve only to demolish any evolution that has been completed at an individual or collective level characterize those who have taken the Esoteric Path and walk peacefully and with as few dis-tractions as possible in the direction of Divine Ascension, not failing to generously offer their own Spiritual Gifts and to lovingly care for the Enlightenment of their fellow men - as much for those who follow them, as for those who act in full or partial Ignorance.

Here we must State and Clarify that Margiori's work has a Clear, Pure, Autogenous, Mystical Personal Point of View, for "every" Earthly-Human - Historical - Ar-chaeological - Social - Cultural - Philosophical - Religious - Metaphysical – Mystical Matter and has NO RELATION WITH nor does it condescend to or is interested in having any relation with any type of Heresy or with new or other

Religions and para-religions. Simply and humbly, with His free-philosophical transcendental work, he completes and extends our Knowledge and ascends our vibration to the beyond, for those who want to learn more about the bottomless Depth and the unfathomable Height of the Creation of the One, but also for those who wish to one day be properly prepared in order to be capable of they themselves becoming His companions.

Although Master N. Margioris was a preeminently Christocentric and Christocratic Mystic, he was familiar with other kinds of Mysticism, such as Free Philosophical Mysticism, Hindu Mysticism, Egyptian Mysticism, the Mysticism of the Ancient Greek Tradition and many others (Paul, Apostle to the Nations tells us about it " **Do not** put out the **Spirit's fire, do not treat prophecies with contempt. Test everything. Hold on to** the good. Avoid every kind of **evil**", to the Thessalonians V 5:19-22), about which he expressed himself and presented his deeply sound Views and Judgments (see his work of three volumes *Mystical Teachings*; *Christocentric and Christocratic Mysticism*; *Theurgy Teaches the Eternal Way of the Soul, Patapios, the Humble, the Philosopher and Saint from Egypt*; *Raja Yoga*; *The Secret of Hatha Yoga*; *Kriya Yoga*; The *Eleusinian Mysteries*; *The Pharaohs Akhenaten and Tutankhamun;* his essays, the *Esoteric Keys*, his journal *Omakoio* and others.)

But the one he always held as Irrefutable, Prototypical and Irreplaceable was the Christocentric and Christocratic Mysticism that he had Experienced and Served since his childhood, obeying His orders ("...and I no longer live, but Christ lives in me..." To the Galatians, 2:20) and the Supremacy that Possesses and Coordinates the Creation as Divine Word ("For no one can lay any foundation other than the one already laid, which is Jesus Christ," Paul to the Corinthians I, 3:11).

Certainly, we do not doubt that there will be some who, in the name of rationalism or in their capacity as experts (academic or religious), will shamelessly attempt to criticize or even to refute a Genuine Work of the Spirit that has been expressed PURELY, in Fullness and in unprecedented Revealing Detail and Coherence by the Christocentric and Christocratic Mystic Nikolaos A. Margioris.

However, SUCH WORKS CANNOT BE JUDGED BY ANYONE ON EARTH (but ultimately, human vanity, human curiosity and interest and the inner need for evolution and to go beyond will touch them sooner or later) and especially with the intellectual functioning that restrictively rules all of us without exception.

Here, we ought to emphasize that if one has not studied His entire colossal and multifarious Work, then one cannot have a balanced and well-intentioned point of view and "judgment" about it.

Unfortunately, all the works of Great men as a rule met with animosity and were desecrated by small men who were not capable of the same Divine Gifts and "were sacrificed" on the altar of the external power and of the rationalistic authority. Paradoxically, and despite their detractors, not only did they survive and become well-known but they were also glorified. On the other hand, when the Pharisees sought his assistance, even Gamaliel (the Rabbi/ Master of Paul the Apostle) told them not to persecute the Christians because if their actions are of God (true), sooner or later they will prevail, while if they are of men, they will be overthrown.

I. L. K.

A NECESSARY CLARIFICATION

Having read many editions that have been published lately both in Greece and abroad and which try to elucidate and to interpret, according to the powers of their writers -but as a rule rationally and anthropocentrically- the legendary Apocalypse of John and mainly to identify it with events in the near future that may occur and that have the "general destruction of the world" as their reference point as well as "the world's enslavement by the Counterbalancing Power (the Devil)" -as if it were not already under his power. We find a juxtaposition of "ample evidence", numbers and indications that attempt to align the Apocalypse to their own points of view and ideas (which, as a rule, are governed by a totally earthly-rationalistic explanation without, most often, any trace of metaphysical orientation, or atleast some metaphysical concern, or they may even be imaginary plots that combine true and imaginary facts in order to arrive at unfortunate and untrue, or partially true, conclusions, which, however may have a significant influence and a detrimental effect on the orientation of our fellow men), which is always dangerous and misleading.

Because all these prophesies, with few exceptions, as is normal, impress the common man who has no particular Philosophical-Esoteric-Theological Knowledge or any relevant Esoteric Education and cannot discern the real from the deceptive, causing him to be deeply concerned, and in our opinion, misguided about the future and overcome with anxieties and phobias. However, the most important, the most disagreeable and perhaps the most dangerous result that emanates from this scenario is the fanaticism and the intolerance that are born of such a blind acceptance of the belief that he-they are the select of God and that everybody else is far from the Truth and also that future events irrefutably depend on his-their subjective and matter-centric "predictions", which may have some very malevolent personal, and by extension, interpersonal, social and spiritual side effects.

Only Free Spiritual Thought, an Esoteric Education, Contemplation, Meditation, Mysticism - which is the ability to penetrate behind the Veil - can allow an evolving being to form "images" that approach the deeper folds of the Visions of such Divine Beings as Apostle John and indicate to him that the described Truth is and concerns innermore Situations-Mysteries of Human Existence and the Creation of God.

Also, very Few human beings who appear in our days and who were not absent from previous times have this noble and highest of privileges to experience and sometimes to witness also in public the same or even higher mystical states during which they hyperintellectually conceive the happenings of the Spiritual Worlds, as well as the Commands of the Father, and convey them converted into the common word of their times so that their fellow men may appreciate them and use them to develop their spiritual evolution-drive-knowledge, since they have been made aware of the Truth and the Laws that govern it.

Such a being was John the Apostle who in his times

and with words that were more comprehensible then than they are today - because they expressed the intellectual level of the people of his times - conveyed allegorically (almost enigmatically) a great part of Esoteric Reality.

In our humble opinion, but also by general consensus of all those who know, another such person was Greek Master Nikolaos A. Margioris who, for the first time, presented a contemporary (1913-1933) Liberal—Esoteric, Christocentric and Christocratic Mystical rendition of the Eschatological Problem in modern speech that was converted from hyperintellectual to intellectual, along with his Complete and Full Vision (Nirguna Samadhi - Theosis of 30 days, see the special note at the end of the book) that is recorded in his book *The Birth and Death of the Worlds and the Beings (matter-antimatter-hypermatter, universe-antiuniverse- hyperuniverse)* as well as in many of his 75 works. It is a completely reasonable and accurate account that records ALL the stages of Creation and of the presence of man on Earth, as much during the process of Involution (the descent of the spirit to matter) as during the process of Evolution (return of the spirit to its Fatherly Shelter) in a detailed manner that is to this day unparalleled. It also includes many other details and aspects of the topic that have NEVER before appeared in the forefront.

Therefore, if we do not have such beings who can talk to us Responsibly and IN DEPTH about these Divine Visions or convey to us their own Spontaneous Spiritual Messages, we are destined to remain in mediocrity, complacency and in the untruth or the half-truth, guided to subjective appreciations of an exoteric kind. Sometimes, we may get a taste of the truth, but never the truth itself ("God is a Spirit, and they that worship Him must worship Him in spirit and in truth," the Gospel according to John 4:24), unless in time we become worthy of evolution through successive incarnations (without this meaning that we will secure the best, because most probably we may be pushed to the worst or stay stagnant for long periods, always according to our choices and to our actions in thought - word - behaviour) and after great pain, suffering and sacrifice, we reach the point of enlightenment and become able to function transcendentally as participants in and communicants of the Truth.

But because such a path requires a difficult, serious and lengthy struggle with OUR OWN SELF, it is rare as an experience, because all of us, good or bad, directly or indirectly, have a "natural aversion" to our evolution, as the devil has to incense, because we TOTALLY identify with, are attached and subservient to matter and there we consume all our dynamism, we set limits on ourselves, and we remain substantially neutral, indifferent and aloof towards the grandeur of the Truth that we bear within us and of the transcendental hyper-emotions that accompany it, because we are limited only to its external, low and "unworthy" clothing and to all the impulses and passions that emanate from it.

Our only PRESENT HOPE is to accept EVEN if it is IN THE COMMON TONGUE the GENUINE ESOTERIC EDUCATION offered to us by our hyper-intellectually functioning fellow men who are Beings on a Mission here on Earth, and to enjoy the closest replicas of the Truth that they offer us open-handedly in their converted language, in order to facilitate us in making our COMPARISONS and our JUDGMENTS concerning all aspects and to INFORM us and ORIENTATE us CORRECTLY AND RESPONSIBLY about WHAT Spiritual Evolution is and

HOW it can be ATTAINED. More simply, we are given the opportunity, through the Revelations of the Great Beings, to solve as much as possible the PUZZLE OF THE TRUTH WITHIN US and to make the most correct and the most beneficial choices concerning our spiritual regeneration, which always requires hard and indefatigable work and many sacrifices.

The Cohesion, the Formation, the Continuity, the Rational Sequencing, the Mutual-completion, the Self-empowerment, the Pure and the Spontaneous, the Deep Popularisation, the Simplicity, the Humility, the Self -Sacrifice, the Respect, the Dynamism, the Fullness, the Bottomless Divine Knowledge, the Freedom and the Love that result from the Full Power on Consciousness (the Intellect) that releases the superior, hyperconscious functioning of our Mind are only some of the Virtues that rule and Certify the Greatness and the Grandeur of the Real Works of the Spiritual Beings who have become HIS vessels OF CHOICE, worthy of His Divine Grace.

THE GIFT OF THE HOLY SPIRIT, DIVINE GRACE - ENLIGHTENMENT OR THEOSIS- IS OBTAINED BY THE WORTHY. IT IS NEITHER GRANTED NOR TRANS-FERRED to any ill-intentioned or even well-intentioned man. Only the struggle with ourselves and the control of our passions can render us really Worthy Vessels of His Choice. Otherwise, we simply trouble ourselves about numerous other things, while all we need to do is focus only on one or perhaps, depending on our evolution and our struggles for ascent, the time has not yet come for us to become the suitable vessels for His reception, so we are either in the process of our Involution (of our complete embrace and identification with the matter-dividing-devil and its derivatives) or in the process of our Evolution (we are beginning to become interested in our spirit, to walk with the spirit and leap with the spirit and perhaps serve the Divine Plan in spirit).

NOBODY is exempted from the Divine Plan; simply, within It exist and move the evolved beings (those who have Esoteric Knowledge about things) as well as the un-evolved (those who have only exoteric knowledge about things - whatever this may mean and involve). Everyone, WHEREVER HE MAY BE, creates his own future on the basis of the acts and the choices he makes according to the priorities he sets and he certainly gets his just share.

I.L.K.

GENERAL ASCERTAINMENTS ON THE PROPHECIES AND ON THE UNCONQUERABLE* NEED FOR THE ESOTERIC EVOLUTION OF MAN

Since we wish to be consistent, direct and frank about Metaphysical Matters, we ought to clarify once and for all that all the catastraphological scenarios that are constantly being developed lately, as well as the tongues that proclaim an imminent doomsday annihilation of humanity which they identify with The Apocalypse of John, are completely outside the Realm of Esoteric Reality and they do not correspond in the least with the Truths that the Apocalypse describes.

On the other hand, without wishing to take on the role of Cassandra, we feel the need to point out that due to the end of the Second Millennium and the Advent of the New Age and the Third Millennium, we seem to be expanding into a new universal, unprecedented and unique landscape, with events unravelling around us at incredible speeds, a frenzied pace, with successive changes, modifications and multiple rapid alterations in every field of action without exception, causing the average man as well as the specialist to feel lost and incompetent before

---

* Unconquerable: a) Without struggle or fight, unwarlike b) Invincible.

these successive and unusual, momentary, multi-frontal, multi-sided, multi-seated and continual changes that occur and that ultimately create VOIDS and ABYSSES in our Knowledge and our ability to comprehend them even as dim general pictures; while at the same time, we feel every foundation and framework we grew up in, developed and functioned, breaking.

This Opening to the "Unknown" inevitably creates increasingly greater individual and collective CRISES in our knowledge and our beliefs, in our exoteric and low classical education and in our ideals. Thus, feelings of weakness, inability, self-deprecation, insecurity and a need for self-confirmation as individuals, religions and nations (even leading to the violent imposition of our own way of understanding and acting) are created within us. These lead to phobias and anxieties about the future and to inhibitions towards the emerging of a universal consciousness and the exchange of a plethora of facts, feelings, knowledge, ways of thinking and new revelations about and applications for everything we know.

All the different walls we had built around us in order to separate ourselves from all the others are breaking. From within these walls we safely and loftily expounded our views about any given matter, sharing our "wisdom" that, due to radical and successive Changes and New matters unfolding at an unimaginable rate all over the world, we are suddenly losing; because with our defective intellectual functioning (popular, scientific and religious - narrowly dogmatic), we are no longer able to grasp the substance and the meaning of these happenings, to observe them, to interpret, to formulate and to foresee them.

To put it more simply, man "bares himself" in front of these machinations and in order for his esoteric (spiritual) nakedness not to appear, he feels the need to react, to do something (exactly as nearly all those who function intellectually or who are without any elementary Esoteric Education do) to move away from the projectors of the Light of Truth that Call him to get out of his cell and liberate himself from his narrow-minded thoughts and acts and to dare to pull up his sleeves, to undergo self-criticism through a prerequisite reevaluation and rearrangement of his values and of his ideas and to start clearing up and ridding himself of his limited atomocentric ideals.

Exactly here is the turning point, the Crossroads and the Station presenting itself at the turn of the Century and of the Millennium we are entering and that is calling us to take the Step of our own Adaptation - Change to Spirituality, the Start of our esoteric and exoteric Convergence ("the Union of Everything").

Within these limits, man should take on his responsibilities and trace the path of his Ascension, take the Great Decision for his soul-spirit future. However, due to his lack of education and to his substantial Ignorance in face of these happenings (his unpreparedness), he cannot understand the emerging evolutions and he is ruled by the Anxiety and the Fear of the Opening beyond the standards with which he had learnt to live.

It is essential that his adjustment to and his actions in the new exoteric events take place with the fewest possible losses, with the help of an objective balancing - connection between his previous knowledge and the newly acquired one as well as the turning Inwards that will solve ALL HIS PROBLEMS, whatever their origin.

In this, one can be helped by the unbiased PURE Esoteric Knowledge (emanations of the perfect mystically converted experiences of an Initiate) that is conveyed in COMMON SPEECH in building his own Internal Center of Weight (or more correctly, to activate the one already existing within him). One should not vacillate or feel harassed or self-limited before the New Opening of Knowledge that gradually becomes more obvious due to external Events and Universal Changes that in various ways surround, provoke and call us... to awaken us from the torpor and the debauchery in which we have fallen and summon us to play an active and not a passive or reactionary role.

In fact, some internal, spiritual-psychical breezes, some strong winds - typhoons are blowing within all of us (the intensity and the extent vary according to our individualized case) and on the Planet Earth. For this reason, man feels lost because he is not yet properly prepared (nobody prepared him) for any change he is required to make not only on an external level but, more importantly, on an internal level.

Therefore, this question arises: Will all of us prove to be a worthy Vessel of His Divine Grace? Will we Dare make the Changes that correspond to us? Will we have the respective spiritual PREPARATION AND DETERMINATION to dare make the small or great Transformations in ourselves and in the world? Will we respond to the Call of our Inner Self and the Divine Orders? How, in which way and to what extent?

These are the inexorable Questions of every serious-minded and responsibly functioning person who apart from himself thinks of others as well; of the embrace, the closeness, the coexistence, the composition, the joint journey, the exoteric and especially the esoteric union (although each of us must preserve our separateness and independence and disposition) of Humanity.

In our humble opinion, those who will Dare, with the pre-requisite assistance of a Spiritual Guide, to embark on their Reconstruction, their Spiritual Regeneration, will find themselves properly prepared and spiritually advantaged when confronting the "New Age" that is knocking at our door.

On the contrary, those who will not move forward and who will remain stagnant, will be wrapped up once more in the arms of their master, matter, and it is they who will constitute the axis-tube of Reaction, a reaction of every kind and form and in proportion to those who have dared, the scales of the future between the Good (spiritual evolution - perfection) and the Evil (materialism and material identification - stagnation or retrogression) will be balanced.

Here, everybody will be called forth to take a stand and shoulder his responsibilities. Depending on the inclination of the balance that will result from the two basic kinds of people (evolved and not evolved) in interaction with the karmic formations that we created in the distant past with our choices at that time as individuals and collectively, there will be the subsequent evolutions that will define the extent of the cruelty and the intensity of the disgrace of the events that we will witness in the near future.

We hope and are optimistic, always respecting the Freedom of every man's Choice, but also the Law of Retributive Justice (see the books *Karma, Reincarnation, Light in the Darkness* and *Raja Yoga* by Nikolaos A. Margioris) that we are living in times where a NEW CREDIT OF TIME has been given (whatever may happen in the meantime) to the souls for them to walk toward the Spiritual Path. However, EVERYTHING WILL DEPEND on our Karma and on our Readiness to correspond to the Orders of the Divine Calling...

On the basis of everything we have expressed above, it is no longer difficult for us to discern that nowadays we are witnessing a More General Universal Turning Point – on many levels of human activity (physical, sexual, sentimental, intellectual, - egoistic - economic, social, political, scientific, cultural, religious, philosophical, spiritual) and it constitutes an almost natural consequence that there will be the necessary – to a smaller or greater extent - natural disruptions and a new order on Earth (geological, seismogenic, volcanic, environmental, an outbreak of new physical phenomena such as El Nino and its sibling El Nina, potential meteorite falls etc., many of which have already taken place) and changes that are even more evidently due to the human factor (increased pollution on Earth, overpopulation, an outbreak of nationalism and religious fanaticism, local or more general upheavals that may become more widespread...).

However, all these and anything else that may appear on our planet and especially in the larger area of the Mediterranean Sea but also beyond it have a double meaning, content and value.

On the one hand, they are the consequences of our own past actions, and on the other hand, it is imperative we find the requisite balance by admitting the "products of our wrong choices", by preparing ourselves essentially in spirit and not only physically and finally, by making new solid spiritually-minded choices, which means that the last phases of this balancing must be driven by our inclination to set ourselves free and not by our tendency to remain chained to the same things, in new captivity and self-imprisonment within the hard stone walls of matter.

The multi-sided external Provocations of the Internal Liberating Currents that touch and cross our Earth from one end to the other, cannot and must not leave us inactive and indifferent or permanently reacting in a sterile and often dangerous way, counter to the Divine Plan. Here we will be judged on our creativity, our Healthy intellectual functioning, the Spreading of our conscience, our Sincerity in Action through the manifestation of kind and superior feelings and Virtues (Love) that we are supposed to have or are developing, and our Struggle for a greater Convergence - Composition - Co-existence, Co-evolution and ESO-COURSE.

We have to Open up outwards and -ABOVE ALL- Inwards, always in moderation, with the help of reasonable and Responsible Guidance in order for us to do right and respond to the obligation we have to commune with our Unknown and Secret Internal Grandeur, with our Internal Unrevealed until now Self, and with the Invisible Side of the Creation that surrounds us, the Divine Will and the Divine Laws that direct it.

We must not allow ourselves to be carried away by our low instincts and by any of our passions or beliefs, to react blindly and retreat to the cruel self-preservation and to the thousandfold repetition of the commonplace and ragged and gaudy earthly ideals, creating a new Karma and obligations that we will be called upon to pay "in cash", but also with the loss of the Spiritual Gate (Opportunity) that opens in front of us.

We should expend no effort on the narrow, single-minded preservation of our bodily integrity and of our ego due to our fear of the Unknown, of the Imponderable and of any ominous "prophetic announcements", for this effort contains none of the healthy elements of the Opening and of the Unity among the People and it ends in an additional factor of restraining everything Good and every personal and collective Evolution, resulting in the respective consequences.

One need not have special training in the "Prophecies" to conclude what we mentioned above. A rational appreciation and a correct reckoning of the current events on Earth, as well as definite ascertainments that derive from the Monocracy of Anthropocentricism and the slavery of man's rationality (everywhere on Earth) are all we need for man to realize (foresee), that we are "fatally" driven to disagreeable and perhaps painful evolutions for the human race and for our Planet.

However, in essence, these unfavorable evolutions (small or great) are our necessary purification - bodily, sentimental and psychical, individual and collective - which may take place at a more severe level than today, which means that man, human activity, has put his hand and has disturbed "inanimate" Nature and its Order, as much as animate existence, and the time is coming for him to pay for a part of the disturbances, according to how and to what degree it corresponds to each of us (we shall reap what we sowed).

Only in this way will a new course of Evolution and Hope for the Spiritual Rebirth of more people on our Planet open up. And it appears that especially in this New Age, the beginning of the Third Millennium, after the filtering of the people and of the Earth, it will give us the spark for the presence of evermore conscientious people, more suited and more ready to pursue and to walk the Path of their Spiritual Regeneration and Self-sufficiency (see Ilias L. Katsiampa's book *From the Master's Mouth to the Student's Ear: With a thorough 400-word glossary of Sanskrit for the students of Yoga* -3rd and 4th essay).

But let's get back to the "game-scenario" of catastrophology that is lavishly played out. We must know that, as a rule, it is very cost-effective and therefore, because of human nature, very profitable.

This means that the human race is relatively easily taken in by the apparent truth of doomsday judgments that accompany current "prophecies", resulting in the shepherding and the reinforcement of Free Will and the way of thinking of the majority to the creation of evolutions similar to those of the above scenario, because the total of these human energy currents are directed at forming these suggested events (creation of negative thought-forms that unite and multiply, pushing humanity to its partial or total materialization).

Anyway, to avoid any misunderstanding or misconception regarding what we are saying, we would like to clarify that our only purpose for presenting all we do is to bring the true Esoteric Dimension to the surface and to "intertwine" all those facts that most people are either unaware of or do not take into consideration (because they interpret everything rationally), or, due to a partial comprehension of them or to the non-existence of any Esoteric Master, falsify, creating combinations of real and imaginary facts. Or, they are attached to the "exquisite" - supposedly - visions, that happen to appear unannounced and depict subconscious (and not hyperconscious) elusive pictures from the "future", that are however of little - and most times of misleading - value, because many parameters that coexist and that are not visible at the given moment of the said fact are not taken into consideration.

And now, to be more accurate, due to the continuous series of doomsday scenarios and prophecies that for hundreds of years the people have been creating in their imagination, a lot of similar thought-forms are created in our adjoining dimension. They depict destructive events for our earth and many of our fellow men who are ruled by the subconscious attraction of these specific dark imaginary pictures and consider them as given, because they do not have the criteria to verify or to contradict all that they conceive they hurry to reinforce these thought-forms, solidifying them with the oral or the written word and urging others to reproduce them.

With this work we wish to gain as much information as possible (hyperconscious -full light- and not subconscious –half-light-) so that we may be able to see things from a Clearer and More holistic SPIRITUAL point of View/Seat and not become attached to body-worshipping obsessions (prophetic or other) and have our future depend on the various prophecies that are fed to us. We have to define it by creating it starting NOW. The TODAY and the NOW have their Greatest Value and Importance and everything depends on how we develop them SPIRITUALLY and not on the insipid and misguided focus -attachment to a preparation for the proclaimed -probable or not- destructions that keeps us in an stance towards life that is completely untrue, misleading and covertly strengthens our lower self of external matter (the body gets its Highest and Real Value when it is directed by the Spirit and not vice versa).

Therefore, great attention and prudence is recommended during the "revelatory" presentation of future events (and especially those in the near future), first because there is no Absolute Future as we perceive it or as we imagine it; second, because to a certain extent, there can be a negative influence of the Free Will of our fellow men whose thoughts are easily attached to the bad or superficial spirituality; and third, many are the factors that co-exist and have to be taken into account before some-one can talk with certainty about future subjects (which in any case is considered to be "forbidden"). It is not only Karma, the obligations of the individuals and of the nations-states or of the Earth as a whole that will defi-nitely be paid, but also the Individual Wills of our fellow men that may, more or less, change even at the last mo-ment and bring the sunrise of the future. Even the speed with which the Divine Plan will be applied is subject to the peculiarities and to the oddities of our choices (we are made in His image and likeness).

Only the Great Initiates can talk to us responsibly about the future. But they usually do not do so because they do not want to use autosuggestion on the people, unless they have received Special Orders – the Authority to reveal small or large parts of the Whole General Divine Plan, for a special reason; perhaps due to the suitability of the times for the General Enlightenment of Humanity, and certainly not to warn of isolated - partial or more gen-eral - destructive events (nor to satisfy our earthly body-worshipping interest - curiosity in an attempt to main-tain and preserve our physical bodies) which either way constitute successive and inevitably "necessary" points of friction (karma, from which we cannot sidestep, we will rebuild what we have demolished) in the historical course of the human race. Of course, Initiates of such greatness and range can be counted on one hand on Earth and they ALWAYS COMPLEMENT, NOT TERMINATE. Moreover, they are WHOLLY consumed by their mission to elevate, even slightly, the spiritual level of Humanity and certainly not to reduce it or to keep it as it is, thus strengthening the existing material bonds and passions that overpower all of us without exception.

Consequently, it is wrong to convey futurisms, which are then re-conveyed (our Master used to say that two things spread rapidly: viruses and rumors), and which gradually compel us to give particularly weighty importance to everything "foreseen for" the future because, as we explained, it contains many (karmic) dangers; first for those who commit these wrongs, with or without particular knowledge about the future, and also for those who induce people to Cassandric thoughts that affect their Free Will, exercising psychological pressure-violence on them to gather closely around the established class and their sterile and fanatic reaction against every evolution and opening; or to enter the camps of the "futurists" who, as a rule, reinforce one-sidedly - willingly or unwillingly - a body-worshiping attachment - and not a spiritually-governed focalization - and strengthen the bonds of the soul within us, so that some smart alecks can "make a living".

Once more, we wish to make clear that The Apocalypse of John has NO RELATION to any prophecies or material visions or rational approaches and so on... that connect it directly or indirectly with doomsday scenarios or other events of the near future. It is exclusively and solely related to the Rendering of the General Divine Plan of Holistic Expression (in all Dimensions) to our Physical Dimension, of the Presence and Withdrawal of Creation from one end to the other (the dissolution) that will take place after millions of earthly years.

On the other hand, we must not forget that when we unswervingly** seek the One Truth, everything else (of

---

** Unswervingly: Unbending, strict, not changing his course

secondary value and importance) will be added according to Divine Distribution ("But seek His kingdom and these things will be added to you").

Only He Knows, Only He Understands and Determines, according to His Laws (Karma) which govern Creation and the ACTS of every man, of every case (individual or collective, peaceful or belligerent) who must survive or not (regardless of the safety and survival measures that have been taken or that are being taken by those who are concerned) and in particular, who deserves His spirituality.

The Spiritual Knowledge that ONLY THE WORTHY possess is SUPERIOR TO any natural disasterbecause man, with its help, Recognizes himself, is Reborn and starts to steadily turn towards his psychical grandeur and to perpetually commune with Eternity. Consequently, he is no longer touched by any physical degeneration and any material imperfection. Man soars over. He is INSIDE the world but NOT of the world.

Vivekananda, the Indian Philosopher who at the end of the past century first brought to the West and popularised the basic kinds of Yoga (that are of Pre-Hellenic-Dravidian origin and invention, see Margiori's book *Dravidians, the Ancestors of the Greeks*) and the Philosophic Systems that accompany it, says that "Spiritual Knowledge is the only thing that can destroy our misery for Ever. Any other knowledge satisfies the necessities only temporarily."

I. L. K.

THE APOCALYPSE OF JOHN
AS EXPLAINED BY
NIKOLAOS A. MARGIORIS,
THE SPIRITUAL MASTER

A BRIEF BIOGRAPHY OF JOHN THE APOSTLE

St.John's vision from a scene from the Apocalypse (1595)
- icon at the Monastery of St. John, in Patmos.

John the Apostle is the author of the fourth Gospel and probably also of the Apocalypse that is estimated to have been written in 95 AD on the island of Patmos, where he was an exile during the sovereignty of the emperor Domitian. He was one of the 12 close students of Jesus Christ and a witness to His crucifixion and it is he, along with Petros and his brother Jacob, who guided the first Christian Community.

John the Apostle has also been characterized as and called the son of Thunder, of the Word. In his Gospel, although he omitted to write about the Last Supper, he presented us the Living Bread, delivering us the Deepest Spiritual Message of His Vibrant and Direct Communion with Him, having Mysticism as his Infallible Guide.

In his Apocalypse, we see the unfolding of the hyper-biblical prophetic visions of destruction and of the Opposition endeavoring to prevail, but with the Thesis (Jesus Christ) as the final victor. These visions concern one and sole event, which is the Visionary Conception of John and its symbolic (enigmatic) anthropomorphic rendition to the people of his times of the very distant yet certain phenomenon of the shrinking of the Worlds and the Beings (the Divine Plan) and of the reaction of any form-matter (Satan) to its expected dissolution and decomposition (the End of Time), which, however, following the Divine Law, will ultimately dematerialize and will return, along with all His Beings, to the Fatherly Arms.

REMINDER

We remind the reader that he is holding a Metaphysical text in his hands, which naturally follows a different and much deeper way of thinking, examination and presentation of events (physical and metaphysical, often completely different from the one we are familiar with) compared to what we are used to in our daily reasoning. This means that the reader must be prepared for a different way of thought and perception, which may be simply written, but is not always understood or credible, because one must succeed in piecing together the PUZZLE of Truth within him before he arrives at any definitive conclusions.

This requires many years of study and persistent effort and, from a certain point on, the apprenticeship by the side of a responsible man who knows the Innermost is indispensable. Otherwise, his success will be limited to an initial, elementary and, as a rule, deficient or highly academic approach not only to the current topic of analysis, but to any truly Esoteric matter which may be examined.

The decodification of Esoteric Knowledge may be presented by Master N. A. Margioris in a simple manner, but it, does not cease being multi-levelled, many-sided and complicated (see the epilogue) and as it gradually becomes understood, every metaphysical word, every relevant meaning, however simply it may be projected outwards, contains within it successive layers of hidden knowledge and of revealing details that we will never manage to exhaust completely with our reason alone. However, with the help of an Instructor of Esotericism, we can certainly be guided to a high level of Cohesiveness of the "Dispersed" Spiritual Knowledge (that comes from an Initiate) and led to form, for the First Time in our life, a Representative and almost COMPLETE PICTURE of the ONE TRUTH as it appears within us and outside us and on the basis of this, we may proceed with greater safety, solidity, accuracy, seriousness and consistency on the Spiritual Path.

Simultaneously with our theoretical development by the side of an Esoteric Instructor, it is self-evident that we also need practical guidance (*From the Master's Mouth to the Student's Ear*) and mainly the APPLICATION of all the spiritual exercises we have been taught either on the Esoteric Scientific-Philosophic Path, or the Gnostic Path or the Religious Path or even through a combination of two or more paths.

Thus, only after much pain, suffering and a gradual detachment from our material covering - dependence, will we be guided IN LIFE to our OWN REAL MYSTICAL CONCEPTION of what all the preserved texts (modern or old, religious or philosophical) of the GREAT beings present to us; of the Spiritual doings within us (which at the moment we are communicating, are possessed and covered by our attachment to the exoteric) which they urge us to sample; and we will be guided not to believe in a completely blind way, but to witness the Truth that ALL OF US bear Within Us for ourselves.

It is this we wish for anyone who approaches the SPIRITUAL PATH with the respective spiritual inclination, responsibility, seriousness, respect, patience, insistence, discipline, self-denial and dynamism.

We remind you that the explanation of the Apocalypse of John by Master N.A. Margioris which follows comes from the transcription of his oral teachings to the written word and concerns its most important and the most deeply symbolic points. Most of the explanatory clarifications that are in parentheses have been made by the writer.

We wish you a pleasant and fruitful read...

I. L. K.

THE APOCALYPSE OF JOHN
AS EXPLAINED BY
NIKOLAOS A. MARGIORIS,
THE SPIRITUAL MASTER

The described pictures of the Apocalypse suggest a world that is in the distant future, that cannot occur here in the Physical Life - Matter. It shows a Perfection that takes form in a Superior World. However, in order for these meanings to be conveyed in our own world, they need visual presentations that address the Mind.

What takes place, in essence, is the Impression of the Being of Perfection on the common Mind of man in order that he may be informed about the spiritual movements....that he may get an idea about the non-depicted. It concerns superior vibrations from the opposite bank of Creation that usually appear on our Earth in the form of symbolic images.

Only an Initiate can correct the voids, the defects or the mistakes (depictions) that occur during the rendition of the vision of an Enlightened being into the common word.

Everything we read in the Apocalypse is a momentary presentation of the superior Dimension that appears to the Initiate at the speed of its vibrations. But in order for these to be processed they need pictures, a series of pictures of our physical world, so that we can comprehend their secret meaning - a meaning that in this Dimension comes from the Instantaneous conception of an elevated Mind.

THE THRONE IN HEAVEN, CHAPTER 4

It concerns a small spiritual movement that he describes in a few sentences. The 24 Priests are the Divine Dynamo-energies. These Dynamo-energies, which are Spiritual, appear in our world in different colors and pictures.

The four animals are four Dimensions. They are large masses of Spiritual Energy and their psychical coating created by the Father. For no Spiritual Energy can distance itself from the Father if it is not covered by a secret Substance that it extracts and is called the soul.

The Power of the Spiritual Authority that is dispersed throughout Omnicreation is coated with a Substance of its own (secret) that is called the soul. While it is descending, this kind essence (spirit) feels the need to protect itself with a protective system-thorax that is called the Soul.

All these beings that John describes concern situations of this kind. They take on a morphic formation so as to be perceived by the Mind. This morphic formation that is perceivable contains nothing more than Perfection, the Soul and the Spirit, as its exterior coating.

This morphic insulation is a result of the esoteric vibration of the Spirit and the Soul. And the ornaments that he mentions are the vibrations of the Spirit to different points (six wings). They are the points from which spiritual rays are diffused (eyes, etc.)

The 24 priests are 4 X 6 = 24. They are dynamo-energies

of God. It reveals to us what occurs in the other Dimensions as well as in the Mind of man (macrocosm and microcosm).

The 4 animals are the 4 symbols of the Evangelists that show the evolutionary state of the human race. It addresses people and they must comprehend it in its human color. John tries, through natural pictures, to show what is unperceived and invisible, what is beyond time, place and causality. These 4 symbols show the spiritual comprehensiveness, the quality that acts on the physical world and forms vibrations for those who can perceive them (Taurus or Earth, Lion or Water, Eagle or Fire, Man or Air). They are Vibrations of 4 kinds in the world of form. Thus, in this simple way, he gives us an example, a demonstration that the eagle moves more quickly than the lion, which means that it is of a higher vibration and value.

We know that these four elements – symbols, in the view of Esotericism, represent the evolving hierarchy of the materialized worlds. So, Earth represents the ox (cow, calf), Water represents the Lion, Fire substitutes for the Eagle and Air represents Man.

Let us desymbolize them with the knowledge we have today, with Esoteric Truth as our companion.

Earth is the anchor, material immobility (slow palm-vibration). It is the basis of eternal principles, of stability and of loyalty to these. It corresponds to Taurus (the ox) and is paired with Apostle Luke, the West and stability.

Water is movement and our rightful search for knowledge of the invisible. It is power, sentiment itself, the Lion from the mouth of which water always runs. The Green Lion means matter and the Red Lion means spirit and it is paired with Apostle Mark, exaltation and the North.

Fire is Knowledge and Spiritual leadership, the power

to create and to recreate all of matter. It is the energetically expressed Spirit. It is symbolized by the Eagle and it is paired with John the Apostle, initiation and the South.

Air is our physical intellect that lives eternally when it is supplied by our internal spirit. It is our inclination towards ascension in order to receive the necessary energized spiritual power. It represents man and it is paired with Apostle Mathew, knowledge and the East.

So, Earth is the Will and the Bull is matter, sensations, the low belief of narration and response, as well as Luke the Evangelist, the solid, the immobile being examined, stability.

Water always cleans and brings the flow and great mobility. Its symbol is the Lion with its known impetus that looks like the waters when they rush forward. It is Mark the Evangelist. Mark is the Lion, high sentiment.

Fire is Light, Knowledge, the Spirit, the Eagle and is symbolized by our wonderful John the Theologian. Because he himself used the Light, the Word; that is, the Divine Spirit. John is the son of Thunder, the spirit, the well-known Eagle of our world.

The Air or wind symbolically means the human intellect. This enters like the wind, without ever being felt by us in the Occult and the Rituals. It is the person who seeks every opportunity to learn. It is Mathew that fully represents this person. Mathew is Man, the Intellect, the pursuit of Occult teaching.

It is certain that Initiate John knew, and of course symbolically taught, the esoteric and exoteric problems of Omnicreation in his Apocalypse.

John narrates some things that took place in the previous Expression (998th) that according to Esoteric Philosophy (of N. Margioris) will again be repeated after millions of years and in the present Expression (999th).

Whatever takes place in another Dimension has a clear influence on us; that is, the vibrations that come are grounded here. John saw happenings in another Dimension that remained stuck in his mind. They had occurred (and they will be repeated here at a certain moment) and they simultaneously took place also within him, because he conceived them, he had psychical sensations.

The fact that we are talking about abstruse transcendental events that a few beings conceive experientially (in a state of ecstasy, a visual conception) does not mean that we will cease to occupy ourselves with them or that we must ignore them. We never ignore them. The view that we should "cease to occupy ourselves with" means absolutely nothing and especially in the area of Esoteric Research. In no case does this thought constitute a point of stability and of progress. On the contrary, by insisting on the perception of these high meanings, we force our Mind to submit itself to psychical nocturnal emissions, thus helping man in his evolution to enter and to identify more easily with the bodiless side of our world.

However, most "experts" who have written the interpretation of the Apocalypse of John disagree with the exoteric, rational view that is aligned with the passage in the New Testament that says "He has made us competent as ministers of a new covenant—not of the letter but of the Spirit; for the letter kills, but the Spirit gives life." 2 Corinthians 3:6. They try to rationally interpret transcendental events that have a symbolic and relative depiction in the writing of John, who describes them. We accuse nobody. But it is one thing to see from the height of a chair, another from a ladder, another from the roof of a building, another from a helicopter, another from a satellite and yet another experience altogether to enter other

Worlds - Dimensions and to live their Truth communicating with the formless reality and being in tune with the Commands of God...

First of all, it would be advisable to carefully study the other Gospels, particularly John's, many times and then to start probing more deeply into the Apocalypse of John in order to increase - raise our vibrations..., to "dissolve form".

In order for someone to introduce spiritual states into the world of form, he must be a great master, a prodigy with the ability to translate spiritual vibrations into natural presentations. This is most difficult and extremely rare. That's why all true Masters guide their students towards spiritual exercises that will allow their Mind to become more distinctive and penetrating, that will activate the superior, hyperintellectual functioning of their Mind so that they will see, with their own eyes, the hyper-reality that exists behind Everything and that in one word we call God.

But the fact is that for one to understand the Apocalypse of John, he must be spiritually evolved.

THE SCROLL AND THE LAMB, CHAPTER 5

The scroll which John refers to is whatever involution (meaning the descent, the falling course - the sinking of the Spirit into Matter) exists in everything. In a seed that will become a big tree, in a baby that will become a mature man. A motionless stone is incarnate energy when, for some reason, sooner or later, it is broken into pieces and becomes lime or whatever other energy is produced again.

The scroll is the cognitive being in evolution. It is the incarnate Mind that is, in essence, the soul, the eternal Spirit. The seven symbolizes the Principles of the Dynamo-energies that will take place. That is, how this book will be expressed, interpreted, explained, understood. It is its wholes, its teaching methods, the seven Vibratory Systems of the Mind, of the Divine Mind and of its conveyance. The seven Vibrations of perception. The same holds for the myths. They contain seven meanings (see N. Margiori's book *The Desymbolism of Greek Mythology*).

The Slaughtered Lamb means the one that is separated from his material formation. We refer to Christ as the Slaughtered Lamb in order to say that he does not belong to any bodily and physical state. He has been slaughtered; his physical state has been detached, though his spiritual integrity remains intact.

The seven horns are Transmitters of spiritual value (Messengers) and the seven eyes are the respective receivers. That is, on the one hand we have the horns whose role it is to transmit spiritual waves - vibrations; in other words, the angels who run and bring the messages. And we, ourselves are the receivers. Guitars, incense, gold bottles etc., are the waves of the angels' formations.

THE SEALS, CHAPTER 6

These visions and the Seals that they open symbolize the spiritual evolutionary states of the human being. That is, the Divine Spark (spirit-soul) that has been incarnated to matter. During the course of its descent into matter, the individualized spirit follows the course of its involution. It is incarnated, covered, wrapped in the darkness of matter and in due time, with the passage of millenniums, after millions of years, it enters the process of its evolution, on the basis of which it starts removing its covers, the clothing of matter that it necessarily wore and it gradually starts to shine.

And John tells us that in the event that the first seal is opened; that is, when the covers are removed and the white horse, which means the most cleansed soul, appears, then he who has the crown of victory will appear. For it is he who has managed to shake off the seeds of matter. That is why the symbolism of the white color of the horse represents the being that is liberated. Because the purpose of man is to develop-evolve from the incarnate state he finds himself in to the halo, the white light, the sun; that is, like his Father.

But in the next seals we see that, in reality, there is a state of semi-purification and that he who appears has a dark color which means that he is not yet evolved, he is on a lower level (here, each person strives to exploit the other or to commit crimes against the other). Evolution has not yet come because by slaying and committing a crime against another, one actually commits a crime against oneself. Because there is but One God and we are his Rays, as indicated by the different physiognomies and mummies. This is exactly what happens in the second seal, the descent begins, the lowly etc. start to prevail.

In the Third seal, as he weighs events, especially those events that concern the monetary currency, on the scales, the amount is the detritus of matter. What is of value has to pass through oil and wine, which means that he has been initiated, he has learnt the Truth, he has obtained Knowledge, and has been released. In other words, on the scales, he is lighter than the other goods of matter he mentions (wheat, barley, wages). In a word, it is the symbolic distinction of the good souls from the bad.

The fourth Seal presents us a more unevolved soul that is typically of a yellow and green color, and shows the fall of man's vibration and presents a continuously declining - from the white of the first seal - downward course. The karmic decision, which is the friction of the man-soul on Karma, follows. It is the payment of the Law that every person is obliged to pay.

The fifth Seal shows us the two kinds of souls: the few evolved ones that are near Him or on Earth, surrounded (armored) by the whiteness of the Spirit and communing with It; and the many unevolved ones that must still suffer many tortures and pains in order to be cleansed of what they themselves created with the wrong course they had taken.

In the sixth Seal, we note that there is a continuous cycle that began with the first and ended with the sixth, where we find ourselves at present. It starts with the bad, the bad multiply, and at some point, the good souls return from the past souls, while at the same time, the vehemence of Divine Justice makes its presence visibly and powerfully known to the unevolved souls that run for cover before the unprecedented events they face.

In the seventh seal, he tries – always in a symbolic manner - to help us understand that the Great Day of the shrinking - dissolution of the worlds will come, and that we will be forewarned by different signs and wonders that will take place. Nothing can remain permanently stable if its shrinkage does not take place.

Certain signs, such as colors or numbers, will warn of this great return to the Embrace of the Father of the Universes that He has created. A time will come when the spreading will cease and everything will turn backwards. Everything will melt.

144,000 SEALED, CHAPTER 7
THE GREAT MULTITUDE IN WHITE ROBES

The 144,000=1+4+4+0+0+0=9 is the ennead system of Pythagoras (see N. Margiori's book *Pythagorean Arithmosophy*) which guides us. It is a system of vibrations and with its vibrations it creates Waves of Life and forms the Worlds and the Beings. 12=1+2=3 is the same, but it is smaller. Behind these, there is Energy. The names of the races are symbolic and concern the Worlds, the living beings. The others, suns - moons etc. are the "unliving" beings that will sustain this Dissolution. All of them will return to their invisible state. The bodies will dissolve.

According to the description, those who belong to God are 144,000 in number (a symbolic number that refers as much to the internal processes that take place as well as to the enlightened souls) and they are sealed spiritually and not in a natural way. More simply, they are the initiated, those who have seen the light and have been reborn spiritually and it is them that the Divine Order counts before the destruction.

The white uniforms symbolize the clear souls, those souls that felt pain and suffered in the world of matter and of form. These souls will be released from all the stigmata of matter they had, they will be purified and they will appear quite pure before the Great Sanctuary of the Father's Throne.

THE SEVENTH SEAL AND THE GOLDEN CENSER, CHAPTERS 8-10

Here, the arrangement of the Worlds and of the Beings that live within them is presented to us symbolically. More simply, John is warning us about the shrinking - folding of Omnicreation (of every living and non-living creature in all Manifestation and not only on our Earth), which will begin from the outside inwards. The seven external Dimensions are symbolized by the seven Angels and the seven Censers that everyone holds in their hands, which are the symbols of Creation and of the Spirit (the Spirit that exists in Matter). The Censer corresponds to the enclosed Spirit of every one of the seven Dimensions.

More specifically, the seven exterior Dimensions ("In my Father's house there are many mansions") that have from very little to a great deal of Matter, start from within outwards, from the Spirit to Matter as follows: 7th, 8th, 9th, 10th, 11th, 12th, 13th (our Physical Etheric one). Deeper still, there are the pure Spiritual Dimensions (1st, 2nd, 3rd, 4th, 5th, 6th) that house only the individual-ized Spirit that, in order to descend from the sixth Eso-dimension to the seventh and then to the other ones, it must emit from within it a Spiritual Substance that, in combination with the superior fine Matter of the seventh Dimension, will surround and will armor the Spirit, pro-tecting it from any material influence. This Substance is called soul and will accompany man during his entire passage through Matter, during his thousands of rebirths, until the time of the shrinking of the Worlds comes again, or before his self-enlightenment, which is attained on condition that he reach perfection; by which we mean that firstly, he realizes his spiritual existence and receives the first great splendors and then, after he is truly evolved and has denied everything earthly and material, however fine it may be, then and only then does he get his spiritual entity again, his Superior Identification with the individualized Spirit that he bears within him and with God.

THE TRUMPETS

The first trumpeting of the Angel announces the beginning of the procedure of restoring everything to the Fatherly Arms from where everything came. The beginning of the dissolution of Creation starts to take place from the outside inwards, from the visible to the invisible, from the 13th Dimension we find ourselves in, the Physical Etheric world (our Physical Etheric world consists of 3/7 physical matter and the remaining 4/7 of etheric type matter, with a total of 7/7). It is this 3/7 of matter (solid, liquid and air) that John describes as one third of the earth, one third of the trees and one third of the grass that were burnt; that is, they began disappearing, dematerializing.

With the second trumpeting of the Angel, as the dissolution of Physical Matter and of the living and "nonliving" beings that live in it continues, we see the shrinking extending to the Astral World as well, the Twelfth Dimension (another 7 states of higher quality matter).

With the third trumpeting, we are given the image of a big star, which is called Apsinthos*, falling from the sky, burning like a torch. While all that is solid is being burnt, so is all that is gaseous; and while the Earth is being burnt, so are the other planets further away from us in our universe as well as in the other Dimensions, and from this a picture emerges of the phenomenon of a "great star, blazing like a torch" which we may understand to mean it came from near us, while, in fact, we mean the dissolution of different heavenly bodies, suns, planets, asterisms, more generally, Matter that comes together to weave a new world. Of course, at the same time, with the third trumpeting, the dissolution of the Intellectual matter of the 11th esoteric Dimension, the Intellectual World, begins.

With the fourth trumpeting the destruction described continues and is obviously extended to the 10th - the Buddhic - Dimension.

* **Apsinthos or Apsinthion**: The grassy and aromatic plant, also known by the names of *Artemisia* or *wormwood*, from which the drink *absinthe* is prepared. The drink *absinthe* is also useful in pharmaceutics. Also, esoterically, it may depict elements of astral-intellectual matter that "direct" or set in motion the dissolution that occurs in Physical Etheric Matter and because of this, some unknown bright phenomena appear in the sky as falling stars.

THE FIFTH TRUMPET

Now we come to the fifth trumpeting in which he wants to tell us that, apart from the shrinking, the distinction between good and evil begins. Those who supposedly have the seal of God are the Superior beings, the Evolved ones, and certainly not just any man with some external mark or clothing.

It concerns souls and the famous seal (it is the high

Esoteric Initiation - Evolution of some souls. The 144,000 is the symbolic and not the literal depiction-representation of the esoterically enlightened beings on our Earth) creates the security and shows the neutrality of the evolved souls towards what is occurring, their ability to remain impartial to what is happening in a Biblical way and is causing all the unevolved and ignorant sister souls (the "sealed" and fully aligned with the Wild Beast - 666 - Matter. Probably, the 666 symbolizes the "sign" that exists Internally in every matter-worshipping soul, the forbidding seal of Esoteric Knowledge that ALL uninitiated souls have due to their material descent and course) to tremble at the thought of what will follow after the natural disappearance of Matter and of its physical bearer, of their "death". The evolved know, because they are Enlightened souls that have communed with the Divine Mysteries and are well aware of what the future brings. In fact, they have been forewarned of what will follow and, of course, they are not worried, they do not die, they do not burn, they do not get ill, are not slaughtered, do not grow hungry nor thirsty, they are the good and the very good souls, the truly evolved souls that are not influenced by any material changes.

On the contrary, the mutable and primitive, the primordial, the black souls will exist at the end of the shrinking of the worlds and will suffer the terror and the fear of the trial and of the annihilation of the flesh. Because the bad soul has a very close relationship with flesh-matter and considers itself to be the flesh and believes that it is everything. In reality, it is insignificant and worthless clothing of the soul. For this reason, the evolved souls remain undisturbed and unparticipating in these cosmogonic events and are not overcome by panic nor ruled by devil-matter – and its derivatives.

John talks to us exclusively about the shrinking of the previous diffused universe of the 998th Opening of Creation that he sees in his Vision, while we find ourselves currently traversing the 999th Opening which inevitably, according to the Divine Plan, at some very distant moment in the future, will have the same fate as the previous one.

Then, after countless billions of years, Creation will be sowed again; the 1000th OPENING (which in Esoteric terminology is called the 1st Circle of Life "Presence-Objectification" of the Deity) will take place and the time will come for it to withdraw, to close.... and then we will pass to the next "Circle of Life", with 1000 more Openings and so on.

Of course, in his effort to render the events that he conceives in visions hyper-dimensionally and hyper-intellectually and not in three-dimensional thought and reason, he creates contradictions and easily misunderstood childish images. However, given the intellectual evolution of his contemporaries (2000 years ago), there was no other way for him to outline and to present these visions and to give a representative picture of what had happened in the distant past and of what was going to be repeated in the far future.

Unfortunately, the Church wore blinkers during the whole affair, because in the years that passed, it allowed many tragic errors to prevail and to predominate over the faithful people. As a result, many of them understood what is described in the Apocalypse of John anthropomorphically - anthropocentrically and completely ritualistically-exoterically, despite the fact that it concerns hyperintellectual events and perceptions whose rendition and their meaning was expressed using common concepts of the time of Christ, from which we are about 2000 years away. Now, our intellectual evolution, our way of thought and the meanings have changed dramatically in comparison with the meanings of those times. What we should do is return to the way of thinking and understanding of those times in order to somehow desymbolize a greater part of the meanings given us, for the Mind of today's man conceives things in a different way than then. This will happen only if an Initiate who can experience the same events happens to cross our path and manages to describe these events with images and thoughts of our times so that they may be comprehensible and logical to a greater or lesser degree, with no misinterpretation, fanaticism, prejudice, identification with other physical phenomena that are unrelated to the Truth that is hidden behind the hyperphysical occurrences to which the Divine Evolution guides us.

What is needed is a lot of study, intellectual practice, a true spiritual evolution; in other words, the shaking off of the matter that surrounds us and, of course, continuous Mind exercises and persistent effort for man to grasp the transcendental Meanings that His worthy children conceive about His Divine Plans.

THE SIXTH TRUMPET

In the sixth trumpet, we see that John depicts the events that will take place during the shrinking of the Universe with particular beauty. Those groups of particles which he describes as dissolving and gathering behind the morphic shapes take on different shapes which after their initial secretion - ejection - extension return to form images that in their semi-formed states are believed by this visionary to form different beings. Beings that have lions' teeth, women's hair, that when struck, produce metallic sounds that resemble the neighing of horses as they go into battle etc.

These are the shrinkages of the elements of Nature; that is, of the atoms returning to the Maternal Arms. Here it should be noted that everything started from the MONO-ATOM, when there was but One Atom which had not released the Golden Egg, it had not yet even released the electrons that transformed it into the element(s) we know it as today. Little by little, with the Power of expansion, a protoforce, which formed the first element, was released from this Egg.

It created a nucleus and an electron that revolved around it: this is hydrogen (an electron) which began to revolve around a nucleus. There is a huge distance between the nucleus and the electron and it is likened to the Temple of Saint Peter in the center of which there is the head of a pin. Between the nucleus and its electrons, an atom contains such great free space.

The creation of a second electron came from the force of an Energy that is divided between body and wave, between mass and energy, which is called Quantum and forms a photon. So, the problem we have to solve is the origin of this Force, which created this property in the atom which enables it to form two electrons from one and to have a second element and others that we know of so far (102 elements - electrons, perhaps more electrons exist that have not yet been discovered).

The Energetic Mind that made this Force, according to the descriptions of John, will now follow a reverse course.

The Energetic Force we referred to will start turning back and the atoms with the many electrons will start becoming fewer and fewer and will follow the process of the complete dissolution of Matter, of its shrinking into the space it needed to be created, of its total demise.

In the same way, the extension of the Universe will take the same length of time, will make the same noise, will go through the same phenomena in order to shrink. In other words, a time will come when everything will be gold, because all the atoms will have as many electrons as gold does. It will reach the point of having nitrogen, salt etc., according to the return to the same (the descending scale).

So, amid the brilliant lights and the bangs and these dramatic phases and the return of liquid matter to its previous basic position, these phenomena that John presents in a particular way will be created so as to somehow be understood.

These are written in the Archives (Akashic Archives - 8th Dimension) and in the Father's Thought. That's why John can see them. They will take place after millions of years.

This translation that is now being made for you is aligned with modern knowledge of Nuclear-Quantum Physics. After 2000 years, I may translate it very differently.

The numbers that he mentions depict the formation of the energies that are working in order to bring things back to their initial position; that is, to destroy the already formed Universe, always according to the Divine Plan.

The smoke is the devastation of the differentiated elements-atoms in the descending scale which, during this conversion from the many to the few, brings a loss of power that is characterized as smoke. The formations into previous elements follow. The way they are made creates fiery shapes restored to a lower stage from which they were in.

The attractive force that compels and deforms them is made of fire. The tails that had heads are different elements that also had the power of retreat behind them, just as they had a head in front that pulled them forward. Now, instead of the knowledge and the current of the wave moving forward, it is turning back, inwards, upwards.

The people (that is, the souls) among all these events that take place, the souls that are bodiless and do not have elements, in other words, that are material atoms that are influenced by rather than being observers of these unpleasant events, see these events as a child sees the houses he builds out of sand and they feel joy or sadness or they become withered or vexed or angry or they applaud or they curse, because they see a tragic event of amassing-shrinking-destruction and the undoing of the plans that the Father had made for them. For a moment, these souls imagine that an enemy of the Father is doing this. But little by little, when they are drawn upwards, they realize the Greatness that is found deeper ...deeper... deeper and then they will grasp that the destruction and the preservation and the construction are all of the same Hand.

The bodiless souls see all these things and cannot yet understand them. They think that it is the doing of the Devil. They do not realize what is happening exactly so they cannot repent. Only when they become absorbed do they see little by little that it is the Plan, the Wish, the Command of the Father that is being executed.

It is the Divine Intellect, the Great Mind that is present and teaches and dictates and instructs and plans all this. But John says it in such a masterful way that they can understand it (that is, he uses a metaphor by poetic licence and transfers internal events to external phenomena, which is very difficult to do).

Some take what he says literally because their mind cannot work to find the Truth. There are also the fantasists who distort and misinterpret these symbolic representations...

THE ANGEL AND THE LITTLE SCROLL

The seven thunders are the subdivisions of the Protoforce (that is of the Father's Thought) that come and in a disruptive manner break into different downward-moving channels so as to bring back the Drained Energy that has made the Worlds and the Universes...

The Joyful Message, the Secret Plan (Divine Plan), these are the Missions of the Father's Thoughts that have Enormous Force. So powerful are they that they can cut ANYTHING in their passage like a diamond spider web. This Protoenergy, His Thoughts, enters the Worlds of Form with such immense endurance that nothing can withstand it and it dissolves everything. Because, essentially, there is no Matter, nor Mass nor Energy, but only a Divine Wave which descends and with the speed at which it comes down it forms amassed amounts of Energy and releases them from within It the moment it is diffused. The mass around us contains the energy within it, and every grain of sand has its own energy that is sometimes converted into energy and at other times it becomes mass, depending on the circumstances and the conditions. However, we know that this conversion of matter from mass to energy comes from a photon, from a Quantum-Wave, which means that it is sometimes a particle and sometimes a wave, spontaneously limited and unlimited and produced by a Vibration of Unknown Origin (it comes from an invisible Center). This is what John is telling us using the terminology of his times (see the book *The Three-Dimensional and Four-Dimensional World* by N. Margioris).

He also tells us that his body, the matter he carries, bears the ordeal of its dissolution, the bitter one. And his mouth, which means his Mind, his head, held the Sweetness of Teaching (the Father's works of Wisdom) and the Enlightenment of the Mind from the soul and the spirit that what is happening is the work of the Father, that above all and behind all is the All-seeing Eye.

The Scroll represents Knowledge, Enlightenment, Divine Revelation that takes place within him and the encouragement (permission) that is granted him to make it known.

THE TWO WITNESSES, CHAPTER 11

The two witnesses are the Energy or rather the Power of the Will, the Angel that glistens and shines like the sun. It is His Power that comes and gives the directions and brings the results of the shrinking of the Worlds. By making these beautiful pictures, he attracts our attention.

The forty two months are the body $42=4+2=6$ $(3+3)$. It is the diarchies of the body until the two opposing forces unite. Bitter-sweet - good-bad - white-black, negative-positive etc. (see N. Margiori's book *Pythagorean Arithmosophy* etc.). It constitutes the physical construction of the body until the two forces that are dispersed within it are united.

The one thousand two hundred and sixty days (1260=1+2+6+0=9) are the nine channels of power that come from above and take all the branches of the Divine Egg it has created and it begins to reunite all the elements it has formed (more than 102 elements) during the shrinkage. It concerns the 9 Protoenergies of the dissolution of the world.

In order to preserve its existence in face of God's Plans to dissolve all, the reaction of Matter at every phase is to form the described impressions of John that culminate in the Wild Beast (666) which ascends from the Abyss (matter).

Three and half days is the symbolic length of time of the struggle that takes place during the observation of the dispersal of the debris of matter.

The earthquake and the seven thousand dead show us the end before the end that is going to take place and emphasizes the gradual shrinking of matter with its reactions and all other relevant events.

That is approximately how things will happen, though not in the same manner and order as in John's vision. According to him, the melting starts and is directed inwards. Seven angels, seven gales. It will begin with the ennead system and it will end with the eptaed and the triad systems. It concerns the height of vibrations.

THE SEVENTH TRUMPET, CHAPTER 11, VERSES 15-19

The seventh trumpet is the seventh branched-grooved Force of Protoenergy that descends. Every one of the seven trumpets has to accomplish its own Mission. The seventh Angel brings Justice with his trumpet; that is, the Perfect Restoration of the elements to their initial position and those that are exposed or react are punished, because they lose their own decisive energy and conform with the great direct line of Divine shrinkage that is completed through these powerful channels (by this time, matter is completely lost).

THE WOMAN AND THE DRAGON, CHAPTER 12

The woman is mother matter. Together with the Dragon, she is the Material existence of the worlds and of the beings (1000th Opening of Creation) that will appear in the future and from which this Baby will obtain the power of Command in order to give back to humanity the courage of its own evolution from involution that matter will have been subjected to. For the Essence to become manifest, a Phenomenon is needed. It must appear as form, as a formation of Essence.

The one thousand two hundred and sixty days (1260=1+2+6+0=9) is the matter through which the Voice and Teachings of our Saviour will once again pass. The war in the sky is matter (Dragon, Mind, Satan, Devil, Apollyon, the Archangel Ilotas, Beelzebub, Adversary,

Counterbalancing Power, Black Prince-Archangel etc.) fighting for its rights.

Also here, clear reference is made to the great blow that the 7th Founding Ray suffered at the level of Eso-dimensions (from its 7th Dimension and outwards, until the 13th) to which we belong (there are 13 Founding Rays-Furrows with their respective -13- Dimensions each. Moreover, every Dimension has 7 sub-dimensions), from the rebellion of the Black Angels with the fallen Archangel Ilotas or Iblis or Lucifer at the head, who 1,500,000 – 2,000,000 years ago created some very tragic events to the outer Dimensions of the 7th Founding Ray. That is what John sees and and what makes him describe them to us with such anxiety and harshness.

Ilotas intended to replace the Spiritual Power with another completely material and dark one. Satan, taking the Free Will from the Good Lamb, made a complete conversion. He wanted to change the course of the Substance (Spirit, Prana) taken from the Father. Instead of sending it to the beings so that they could live in goodness, he suddenly changed this Substance and turned it into a Black material substance of bad quality, with which to saturate the worlds and the beings that lived in these seven lower Dimensions. This came to the knowledge of the White Hierarchy which reacted immediately by summoning the Taxiarch Archangel Michael (who is like God?) from the 4th Founding Ray who together with his Angels undertook to face, and after great battles, to neutralize Ilotas and the armies of the angels that he had infected with the Negative force, which for some time he managed to sow to all the external Dimensions and to the beings that reside there (see N.A. Margiori's book *Occultism-Volumes A and B*; *Mystical Teachings-Volumes A,*

B and C; *The Birth and Death of the Worlds and the Beings* *(matter-antimatter-hypermatter, universe-antiuniverse- hyperuniverse)*; *Posthumous Life,* etc.

He brought the Balance and Order back and it is he (the archangel) Michael now who is responsible for distributing God's Essence of Life to his Creatures in Absolute accordance with the Divine Plan.

Matter was defeated, our bodies dissolved into the happiness of our spirit-souls from the kingdom of God who is Spirit, "God is spirit, and those who worship Him must worship in spirit and truth," according to John 4:24.

The Spirit is the ruler of Matter, the beginning from which it springs and lives. And in the magnificence of this war, the spirit-soul of man also saw its liberation. And the spirit of God hovered over the surface of the waters...

Of course, the Book of Life is the book of the Slaughtered Lamb and from the beginning of the world and throughout it are written the elements of the spirit-souls that come from the Creator of Everything. The spirit-souls of the people were formed by the Eternal before our Universe was made and Man was not made, as Moses says, at the end of Creation.

This is of great importance because it proves the arrival of the souls from the depths of the Esouniverses - Dimensions.

BABYLON, THE PROSTITUTE ON THE BEAST, CHAPTER 17

The scarlet beast and the prostitute symbolize Matter-Form and our lower-external self with all the weaknesses, passions, instinctive primitive impulses of the animal and the defects and pettiness of every kind.

The woman is the soul, isolated and limited within matter (from the physical body and the material representation around her), inescapably imprisoned and enslaved by the superior servant of matter which is the Mind (conscience, cognitive functions) of man and is aligned only with the material-exoteric knowledge on the basis of which she constructs her life. The seven chapters are the seven Dimensions.

THE THOUSAND YEARS, CHAPTER 20

The one thousand years symbolize the Absence of the Divine Being (Pralaya) and the total lack of any Creation (Matter) during this symbolic Period, until the moment when the Creator exhales from within Him a new Manifestation again and the Divine Plan is repeated, and the spirit-souls are sowed again, in order to gain experience in matter and to contribute to the "self-perfectionism" of the Father that is continuously and endlessly taking place.

EPILOGUE OF THE APOCALYPSE OF JOHN

We believe that the General Essential Picture and mainly the Esoteric Meaning of the symbolism in The Apocalypse of John has been understood and that many indispensable Keys were given for further study and for a thorough examination.

On the basis of what - for the first time - was presented above, with the help of Master N.A. Margiori's books *The Birth and Death of the Worlds and the Beings (matter-antimatter-hypermatter, universe-antiuniverse- hyperuniverse)*, *Posthumous Life, Esoteric Philosophy, The Two-Volume Metaphysical Encyclopaedia, The Desymbolism of Greek Mythology*, 49 issues of the metaphysical journal *Omakoio*, in addition to the books *Mystical Teachings-Volumes A, B and C, Occultism-Volumes A, B and C, Christocentric and Christocratic Mysticism, Theurgy Teaches the Eternal Way of the Soul, Pythagorean Arithmosophy, The Eleusinian Mysteries, Three-Dimensional and Four-Dimensional World, The Pharaohs Akhenaten and Tutankhamun, White Magic, Karma, the Law of Retributive Justice, Reincarnation, Raja Yoga* etc., you, yourselves can, by combining the desymbolic meanings, make an effort to interpret the remaining points existing in the text of the Apocalypse of John (and other Esoteric Texts) of secondary character and value that basically concern the individual processes of what will occur at some time in the future.

ASCERTAINMENTS

Our occupation with the Spiritual Life in the last 17 and more years puts us in the unpleasant position of ascertaining - of course, we may be wrong - that the atmosphere surrounding many "Metaphysical Movements-Activities" is not characterized by Pure Teaching and a clear Metaphysical Landscape (Mystical Orientation).

We feel that this phenomenon is a mutual relationship that has, on the one hand, the seekers who have low demands and expectations and on the other hand the people who represent "metaphysics" (or more correctly, parapsychology that appears to be thriving nowadays), resulting in particular interest being given to matters of secondary value and importance, that in no case promote spirituality, nor does it change human nature for the better, elevating it –perfecting it.

To put it more simply, in such cases, no substantial internal change takes place in those occupied with the matter. In fact, we could say they are simply playing with spirituality or they are following the fashion of spirituality, wearing its colors, and sometimes even trading in it, instead of representing it wisely and correctly.

This, of course, is irrelevant and does not mean that there are no conscientious, healthy esoteric, philosophical groups with direct or indirect communion with Genuine Pure Spiritual works. They are few but they certainly do the work they have undertaken seriously and responsibly and are far removed from any parapsychological conceptions, literature and practices that have recently developed to serve earthly and not spiritual needs.

We take it as a given that everyone's Freedom is respected and that everybody can say and do what they like provided, of course, that this freedom is not used at the expense or for the exploitation of others...

Now, on the ecclesiastic-religious part, we feel the need to mention in all humbleness and respect that the teaching of Hesychasm, of the Unbuilt Light, of Christocentric and the Christocratic Mysticism and of Special Spiritual Exercises that must necessarily - together with ecclesiastical life - accompany, if not constitute, the first priority in every Christian's life is not encouraged as much as it should be. As a result, the esoteric conversion of a Christian and his growing closer to the life of Christ is depicted as defective and problematic (see *The Philokalia of the Niptic Fathers* (5 Volumes), The Garden of Virgin Mary Editions; *The Invisible War* by St Nicodemus of the Holy Mountain, Tinos Editions; *Corpus Areopagiticum* by Pseudo- Dionysius the Areopagite; *The Uncreated Light,* by Gregory Palamas and many other relevant writings).

Of course, it is common knowledge that every external intervention for change in the society of man is inherently imperfect and "condemned" to failure because it does not take into consideration the basic inner folds of human nature (the spirit-soul). But when there is Esoteric Cultivation - Education or Mystical Contact (Mystical Life) with a cleric or layperson, any external intervention exerts a deeper and more hopeful and substantial influence.

Fortunately or unfortunately, man must change from within. If this change from within does not take place, then it is difficult for him to achieve his transcendence to the Kingdom of the Heavens or more correctly, his Spiritual Regeneration (the hyperintellectual function of his Mind. The purpose of prayer is "obtained only when the man who prays controls-immobilizes his imagination, not allowing it to wander – move, without allowing it to generate ideas and images, when it is completely devoid of any rational meanings and thoughts." Gregory the Sinaite) and, of course, the creation of a society with a more human face, where spiritual orientation and formation constitute the first priority of Education.

Not a few times did my Master emphasize, among other things, that "Mysticism is the headlight of Religion and the Salvation of the Church. Where there is no Mysticism, there is ritualism... and idolatry", "Mystics are well aware that their fellow men are not at this moment ready to enter the high spiritual vibrations of God, of the Father's Essence, the spiritual conveyance of the Thoughts and Ideas and Wishes of God. That's why they guide the unprepared in the direction of the Church, from which they will obtain their future salvational Mystical Life" "The heresies come to life and appear in the dogmas, in the rituals, in the different-interpretations, in the rhetorical and exoteric manifestations of Piety. In real Mysticism, all these neither exist nor happen nor can take place because there is only One Path which involves FAITH in God and WORSHIP to God and TRUE PERFECTION TO... THE FAITHFUL... Here the words of ritualism lose their strength and what prevails is the holocaust of the EGO through SACRIFICE."

Also, "Allow Mysticism to spread freely and help it because it is the only way for humanity to return to Piety,

Morality, Spiritual (Intellectual) Health and the Peaceful coexistence of all the peoples of the human race."

However, are we not all of us partially responsible for the spiritual goings on and for the opening of the way of our metaphysical course? Are we free of blame concerning this more general problem of the shallow, if not, nonexistent metaphysical quest or course of the world which "breeds" in turn the respective political or ecclesiastical "guardians" and "sovereigns" who determine our fates? Men who are very often content with a sterile preservation and not with the spiritual and regenerative INTERVENTION they should be making on the soul-spiritual, physical and especially metaphysical future of every man.

Until when will we follow the preservation? Until when will we be content with the superficial? Until when will we worship matter in all its forms as God and until when will we confine our true BEING within us?

Perhaps change in society is in our hands.

Perhaps the time has come for ALL OF US to practice self-criticism.

Perhaps, this the right moment for us to think hard about the course that we have selected and about the consequences that we suffer because of it and of the others that follow.

Perhaps the time has come for us to dare to turn toward spiritual things with greater maturity, fidelity and stability.

Perhaps the time has come for us to seek to be formed spiritually?

Perhaps the time has come for us to put into practice (even a little more) the spirituality within us and outside us?

In all honesty and sincerity, we wish to clarify and to

confirm that everything we have written above constitutes our personal conclusions (and our concerns about the future) which, however, we believe are more widely accepted by all those who, more or less, know what there is to know about spirituality, and depict the actual adverse situation we find ourselves in, the crossroads to which we have been led and at which ALL of us are called upon to choose the path we desire, and so create our Individual and Collective Future.

Also, it was our Master's clear directive to make it our goal to spread Esoteric Knowledge to the people open-handedly, always according to our personal powers and to our crystallized points of view (that are the fruits of knowledge that we received from our Master) for the soul-spiritual future and the potential abilities of every man; to make known the Enormous, Many-sided and Unrivaled Spiritual Work of Master Nikolaos A. Margioris, which we are quite certain helps Substantially and shapes Spiritually every serious-minded person, that it contributes greatly to the spiritual formation and creates the preconditions (in our present times) for the spiritual regeneration of modern man.

Besides, whoever so desires has all the time and ease at his disposal to study and judge this Work.

I. L. K.

EPILOGUE OF THE WHOLE WORK

If all these prefacing notes and comments were to be written again, it would certainly be a difficult, laborious and time-consuming task; painful but also pleasant work because it would give us the opportunity to express ourselves more extensively and with much richer words that would add new complementary elements, because the analyzed matter would be examined from new optical angles and folds or would probe deeper into existing ones.

That is exactly what Esotericism or Esoteric Education (Occultism and Mysticism) means. The Insufficiency and inability of the common word (oral or written) to convey the complete, ultimate explanation of all aspects of metaphysical matters. At the same time, it goes without saying that we must continue the struggle to proclaim in conventional terms more and more details and new, unprecedented revelations or deeper analyses of older presentations of the least elucidated aspects that concern the Manifest (visible) and Unmanifest (invisible) Creation and the One Truth, so that the opportunity may be given to everyone concerned, student or seeker, to receive whatever he judges as more useful or that he has a greater need of to ascend a step higher, to somehow awaken his Eso-Being.

The Comprehensible, Rich and Vibrating Spiritual

Food that is rendered by today's vocabulary is what the modern man who is guided almost Fully by his square Logic Immediately Needs.

Only if he is given Substantial answers and an analysis of the Metaphysical Truth that comes from the Transcendental Changed Word into a daily, intellectually sensible word, will he receive the proper Stimuli-motivation and mainly the Knowledge that will Complete and will Stir Awake his sleeping soul-spiritual existence and will gradually give him the opportunity to gain sound and solid spiritual orientation and to receive sight.

On the other hand, the more spiritually evolved one becomes, the more one realizes the infinity of Divine Knowledge and of His Worlds, but also one's smallness in front of the insuperable Magnificence of God.

For this reason, he who studies Metaphysics (the Truth of Everything) continually bows his head and becomes laconic or keeps silent because he realizes that our consciousness is of limited value and range and cannot contain and summarize, however much it may wish to, its greatest facts... And he ought to return to these matters repeatedly in order to readjust, slowly but steadily, the broken pieces of the mirror of the One Truth, that having been shattered, shows that it reflects many and different truths, but when it is united and becomes One and Indivisible, as it was in the past, it reflects the very Ray of Light, of the One Truth intact.

I hope with all my heart that we will all become able to face this Inner Unified-One Truth at some point in our life, without its cosmetics because only then will we find-see our real Self and its direct connection with the Father, NEVER BEFORE.

For this reason, although every Autogenous, Pure

Metaphysical Work has Perfection firmly grounded within it, it does not contain Perfection itself, but the approximately comprehended - through consciousness - Perfection, its perfectly modified depictions. However, at the same time, every truly metaphysical word that is the result of some perfect mystic experience is eternal in our world, everlasting and permanent... Perfect...

A word to the wise is enough and let anyone accept who can...

Do you perhaps grasp the Mystery and our weakness and our ignorance?

We hope that we gave you a first representative (truly spiritual) picture of the Essence of the Apocalypse of John and how it is distinct from other earthly prophecies or interpretations that identify themselves with it as well as the spark that will prompt you to Study the insurmountable work of Master Nikolaos A. Margioris ("It is no longer I who live, but Christ lives in me." Paul the Apostle to the Galatians 2:20, "Follow my example, as I follow the example of Christ." Paul the Apostle to the Corinthians 1-11:1) as well as to re-examine the existing reality and the Truth that all of us will approach of our own will, through frank personal struggles and sacrifices and especially under the direct guidance of the Responsible Guide (clergyman or layperson), Master of Wisdom (if possible, an Initiate) or even an Instructor of Esotericism (see the word Instructor of Esotericism in the glossary of the Sanskrit that is found in Ilias L. Katsiampa's book under the title *From the Master's Mouth to the Student's Ear*).

Trikala, November 21, 1998
Ilias L. Katsiampas
(Omakoio of Trikala)

Master Nikolaos A. Margioris

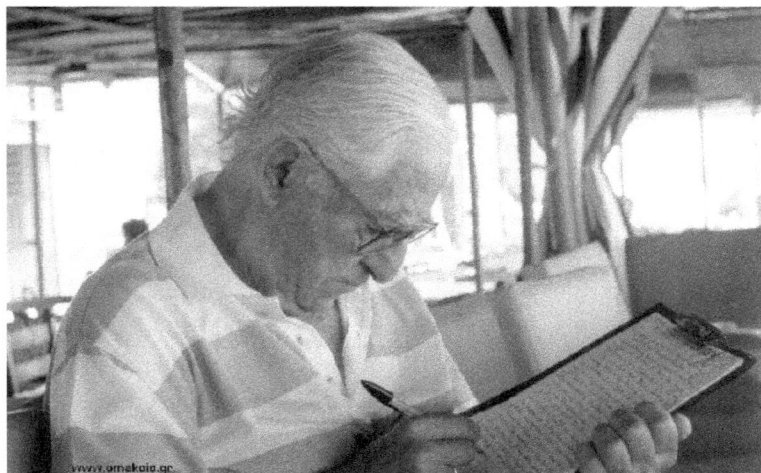

Master Nikolaos A. Margioris as he is writing

BIOGRAPHICAL NOTE
OF NIKOLAOS A. MARGIORIS

Nikolaos A. Margioris (15/12/1913 - 6/5/1993) constitutes one of the greatest and most prominent figures in the area of Esotericism (Occultism and Mysticism). He is not only a recognized, but a fully-experienced Metaphysical Omni-Scientist-Master who was characterized as 'the Patriarch of Greek Occultism' in a relevant interview of the journal *Third Eye*, in its December 1992 issue. This was his first and his last public appearance.

Therefore, this is in memory of Nikolaos Margioris, who was a great Christocentric and Christocratic Mystic and modern Initiate, and we, a group of his closest students who followed him the last few years and were lucky enough to be taught the deep elements and aspects of the Universal Truth, to enrich our Occultist and Mystic Knowledge and to receive a part of the abundant LIGHT that he spread around him, feeling gratitude and sincere, not fanatic Love for him, would like to inform every seeker of the Truth, about the Master's life, personality and work.

Nikolaos Margioris was born on the island of Samos in the village of Vourliotes on the 15th of December, 1913.

When he was 13 years old, he attained Samadhi-Enlightenment for the first time.

He was educated in India and in Tibet for almost 13 years. He lived with his relatives for many years in Alexandria of Egypt where he pursued his studies and made his career. He married Laitsa Papandreou with whom he had two children, Andreas and Kalia. He fought in World War II as a reserve officer in the Sahara Desert where he was wounded in El Alamein and in Rimini. For his services to the country, he was honored with many medals (among them the Big Cross) and with a veteran's disability pension. Also, he was honored twice with the Cross of Saint Mark for his contribution to the Church by Christoforos and Nikolaos the 6th, Patriarchs of Alexandria.

Apart from Egypt, he also taught in Greece from the first day of his arrival in 1958 until 1993, when he departed. He wrote books and essays, he circulated a journal and he created a cycle of studies by correspondence courses.

He considered Metaphysics to be the only Truth and believed that man can attain Truth as Socrates did through his famous MEDITATION (DHARANA-CONCENTRATION) or through Religious Mysticism (Christocentric and Christocratic Mysticism).

All his teachings, his books, his essays, his studies in Esotericism come and emanate from his deep Mystic experiences (Nirguna Samadhi-Theosis).

Since he was very young, he was a participant in these transcendental states which he managed to transform in an incomparable way and to convey to his students and to the world as Knowledge, advice, guidance, for use, practise, training, therapy and personal experience.

His philosophical approaches on Creation, on Truth

(God), on the visible, perceptible and invisible, imperceptible Laws that rule the World and life, in general, are expressed with unique fluency, detail, analysis and depth. He also unveiled new Esoteric Revelations as well as presented for the first time a complete and sound Occultist and Mystic view of the Creation of All, using a torrential and overwhelming form of oral and written expression which rivals, without exaggeration – for anybody who knows - that of Apostle Paul, Vivekananda and Pythagoras, whom no obstacle, sickness, or anything else restrained (he came close to death at least three times).

On the contrary, he believed in the provision of Everything in full, of continuous guidance, instruction and unceasing Sacrifice and the Exemplification of a prototype that can be described in two words "PERFECT MAN AND PERFECT GOD" without publicity, propaganda and proselytism. And certainly with absolute respect for the freedom of every potential seeker.

He was a faithful soldier of our Lord Jesus Christ, a 'TRUE RAVI-CHRIST' and also His imitator, having always followed His Work and His Teachings, reviving it once more in our society of today.

A few words about his multi-dimensional work

After 23 years of Metaphysical publications (1970-1993), he wrote 33 books of clearly Esoteric subject-matter. He also published 33 special essays on different esoteric matters and circulated the first purely metaphysical journal *Omakoio* in our country which included incredible and unprecedented Metaphysical analyses and helped popularize the subject.

He created a field of studies through correspondence courses under the name 'Esoteric Key'. In this field, the students received instruction characterized by a deep, theoretical and practical Esoteric analysis in the following courses: MEDITATION, HYPNOTISM, ORTHOPSYCHISM, ESOTERIC PHILOSOPHY, ESOTERIC THERAPEUTICS, ASTROLOGY-ASTROSOPHY, ESOTERIC INITIATION, SCIENTIFIC SPIRITUALISM, DESYMBOLISM.

Every three months, he held seminars in SHIATSU lasting for many days in which he himself not only taught SHIATSU but a lot of other Esoteric therapeutic systems among which were also his own discoveries whose therapeutic potential is immense and whose success rate surpasses 80%.

Some of his own discoveries which he obtained through personal experience and deep Esoteric Knowledge are mentioned in his books and were taught to his students. They are:

From the LEFT PALM of the hand, he identified the main terminals of certain internal organs of the human body. (N. Margiori's Discovery).

FINGERTAPPING: It is a rapid method of stimulating the whole organism, the cells and the endocrine glands to secrete new hormones and heal the ailing person. (N. Margiori's Discovery).

GLOSSOTHERAPY (TONGUE THERAPY): With special kneading, pulling and massage movements on the tongue that have an immediate effect on the muscular and nervous system and on the whole organism for recovery and therapy. (N. Margiori's Discovery).

HE REVIVED and used the ancient Greek Asclepian kneading-massage method that Asclepius, the father of Medicine, invented and applied in ancient times in the Holy Sanatoriums of Ancient Greece (*Asklepiaia and Amfiaraeia*).

SUGGESTIVE THERAPY through heterosuggestion or autosuggestion. Revival and presentation by N. Margioris.

SLEEP THERAPY or otherwise Hypnotism-Orthopsychism or Technical Sleep - three scientifically complete methods. Presentation by N.A. Margioris.

RELIGIOUS EMOTIONAL REQUEST by the side of the patient. Presentation by N. Margioris.

JAPANESE SHIATSU - Fingertapping (classification of Shiatsu by Master Nikolaos N. Margioris. 186 diseases are classified into 23 groups, each with their general as well as individualized therapeutic methods). Classification and Presentation by N. Margioris.

METHODICAL STIMULATION of all the Endocrine Glands (chakras) for remedy. Nikolaos A. Margiori's method.

BIOENERGETIC INFLUENCE on the 33 vertebrae of the vertebral column for the therapy of 193 diseases of the human body. N. Margiori's method.

STATIC Therapy with the hands-palms. N. Margiori's presentation.

KINETICS Therapy with the hands-palms. N. Margiori's presentation.

REFLEXOLOGY or reflexive zonotherapy. N. Margiori's presentation.

ICONOPLASTIC therapy from near or far. N. Margiori's method.

HECTOPLASMATIC EXHALATIONS OR HECTOPLASMATIC EFFUSIONS- N. Margiori's method.

MANTRAMOTHERAPEUTICS. Remedy with Power words. Presentation by N. Margioris.

TRANSFUSION OF ENERGY, healthy vibrations. Presentation by Master N.A. Margioris.

ATTENDANCE of Litanies or Liturgies.

HOLY ZEAL. The reinforcement of unshakeable Faith in any Ideal or Belief that vibrates man internally and creates the preconditions for the elevation of his vibrations in order to restore his health.

KRIYA YOGA. Method of Somatopsychical Therapeutics. It contains physical exercises-postures in combination with special breathing exercises for the revival - remedy of the body and mental exercises of comparison for the release of man from every kind of repressed emotions, phobias, passions, etc. Revival and Presentation on a universal level by Master N.A.Margioris.

KUNDALINOTHERAPY. Through the exhalations of Kundalini or/and by its awakening.

RAJA YOGA, 8 stages-steps of therapy of the body and of the Mind (scientific-psychological method).

Ethicoplasm of man, therapeutic positions according to the problem, manipulating universal energy (prana) and supplying it to the organism through proper rhythmical breathing for prevention or therapy, retaining the life force that we have within us and preventing its purposeless waste, directing it toward higher purposes, steady concentration on one and only thought-target-ideal for 12", its extension to 144" (meditation, internal identification with the target) and, finally, with the extension of the sole-thought for 1728" we come to the complete therapy of body and Mind, the Union-Enlightenment-Harmony, Full Consciousness of man.

MIXTURE - COMBINATION of many of the above Systems.

These are some of the most important, effective yet innocuous Esoteric - Physiotherapeutic Systems, some of which have been scientifically validated and are taught in universities abroad, while many others are being studied for the positive effects they have on the human organism.

Apart from teaching the Therapeutic Systems, he used to provide therapy, as did those of his students who had been trained. At the same time, he operated a school of KRIYA YOGA where instruction was undertaken by the first female teacher of Kriya in Greece, Mrs. Smaro Kosmaoglou, who had been instructed by Master Margioris himself. He also ran a weight loss school using the system of Atmoliquefaction (his own invention).

He also taught the Genuine and Complete RAJA YOGA, as well as all the systems of YOGA: Hatha, Kriya, Mantra, Karma, Bhakti, Jnani, Tantra (Kundalini), as well as ESOTERIC PHILOSOPHY - THEOLOGY, KABBALAH and ESOTERICISM (OCCULTISM AND MYSTICISM).

He did all his teaching and other activities from his seat in the Spiritual Philosophic Laboratory which was established in 1976 and was called "OMAKOIO OF ATHENS", in memory of the OMAKOIO that Pythagoras created for the first time in Croton of South Italy.

In 1972, he founded the Association "THE PIOUS PILGRIMS OF THE UNBUILT LIGHT, ST. PATAPIOS", where he regularly delivered free lectures on various Esoteric topics.

He was a Permanent and Indefatigable Worker and Guide of the Good and Perfect, a Continuous and Inexhaustible Source of Divine Knowledge.

The above are written as the smallest homage that we, his students, could render him, promising to continue and spread the legacy he left us.

NOTE: The above presentation of Master Nikolaos A. Margioris' personality, life and work was written by his student, Ilias L. Katsiampas (on behalf of all the students he taught during the last decade).

In the beginning, the Master's biography was sent, on the writer's initiative, to foreign guides of metaphysical organizations and to different other metaphysical movements abroad. Then, after the Master's death it was revised and completed correctly by his student and the writer of this book and it was published for the first time in the metaphysical journal *Third Eye* in issue 28 of September 1993, four months after his departure.

Afterwards, it was included in the 3rd Volume of the Master's work *Mystical Teachings* that was published in 1994, as well as in the republished editions of the books *The Other View of Erich Von Daniken's Dogma* and *Dravidians, the Ancestors of the Greeks, The Secret of Hatha Yoga, The Reign of Minos, the Great King of Crete* and *The Chiroplastic Theurapeutics of SHIATSU, VOLUME 3*.

SYNOPSIS OF THE RARE GREATNESS
OF THE MASTER

Master Nikolaos A. Margioris was an Occultist (Occultologist), a Christocentric and Christocratic Mystic, a Modern, Genuine Initiate and Spiritualist.

He is the Master of Masters who silently, prudently and with unprecedented Convergence - Unity - Homogeneity of Work, Autogenous Perfection and a Uniqueness of Revelation and Rendition, exposed to the eyes of his students and to the common experience of every seeker as well as to the whole world (Esotericism for All) the Hyperintellectual (Spiritual) COMPLETE and Perfect Mystic Experiences - Messages of his Soul, his Spirit, of the Source-Truth-God itself, through his 189 books and his teachings.

We could say that the person of Master Nikolaos A. Margioris can be "summarized" in a few words in the following definition:

We are talking about the Greatest (extremely Rare) Esoteric and Greek-orthodox Radiating Personality of such Grandeur, Range, Caliber and prolificity, a creator of a Concise and Pure Spiritual Work that seems to be unprecedented and incomparable in our days, not only for Greek standards but also on a Universal level.

Were someone to attempt to "capture" in written word his preserved oral traditions and his extensive "inexhaustible" dialogues that only we, some of his students of the last decade, know, they would easily surpass the 1000 Substantial Esoteric Works (most of them expressed for the first time and revelatory in nature).

Certainly, were we also to calculate what has not been preserved or what we could not trace or other oral deliveries whose fate we are ignorant of (in Greece or in Alexandria where he lived for many years), then, of course, they are countless (they may surpass the 5000 spiritual works; the number of works that Orighenis is said to have written).

We are certain that future generations will search with particular fervor, persistence, care and difficulty for evidence, fragments, aspects and details of the person and the work of a True Modern Initiate who walked among us and who was SO giving that ultimately the people of the future, being more mature spiritually, will recognize, will "worship" and will follow with great zeal and a feeling of real respect and duty.

The reader can find some information about his person in the only public interview he agreed to five months before his passing, in the metaphysical journal *Third Eye*, issue no. 28, December 1992, where he revealed himself in public.

He who is interested will find two more presentations-reports of his life and his work in some recordings made by the narrow circle of his students in the *Third Eye*,

September 1993, issue 28 (it is published above) and May 1994, issue 35. Some of them are also re-published in his books that were re-edited.

In the book of the director of the Omakoio of Trikala under the title *From the Master's Mouth to the Student's Ear, with a thorough glossary of Sanskrit (philosophical dictionary of 400 words) for the students of Yoga and of the Esotericism* one can find all the above presentations as well as a more recent one.

Finally, in the 3rd Volume of *Occultism*, an important new presentation about the Master is included.

His student, Ilias L. Katsiampas, is working on a more extensive and complete presentation of the life, the personality and the work of the Master that will include even more aspects of his passage through our world and his Esoteric Work that he left as a legacy of Knowledge and Instruction for the future generations who will evolve within the framework of Mysticism (Philosophical, Gnostic and Religious).

REQUEST

Those who were fortunate enough to have directly or indirectly known Master Nikolaos A. Margioris from his early years in Greece or before that when he lived in Alexandria of Egypt or/and in India and who consider that they have additional testimony or more information about his personality and his work are requested to come into contact with us and if they wish, to notify us, so that the new Biographical Note which is being prepared by the director of the Omakoio of Trikala may have greater detail in its analysis of the events of the life and the activities throughout the course of His life, so that his life and His work can be more completely depicted.

A FEW WORDS ABOUT THE 30 DAYS
OF NIRGUNA SAMADHI - THEOSIS
OF MASTER N. MARGIORIS

First of all, we should mention that Master Nikolaos A. Margioris had some Esoteric Experiences when he was very young. But His first Complete Theosis - Enlightenment took place when he was 13 years old. Throughout the course of his life he often experienced Liberated Mystic Ascensions-Experiences which lasted from very little or extensive earthly time.

However, the longest one in duration and the greatest in Esoteric Spiritual Completion was the one that lasted nearly 30 days, during which he not only traveled the entire Esodepth of Creation, with the help, accompaniment and guidance of Jesus Christ through whom he was able to approach the Inner Darkness of the Father, but also remained, within the place-time limits of the 30 days, in continual Contact with and the recipient of Supreme Knowledge and Wisdom concerning the Divine Meaning of Omnicreation, the highest Beings that supervise it and the General Divine Plan which Commands and Preserves it from one end to the other.

During this Complete Integration - Brilliance - Theosis - Blending with the Divine Hyperreality, he conceived the

One Hypertruth of All and the way in which it "splits" Its Powers "Exhaling" Omnicreation, the Laws with which it Supports it and the Beings that look after it, the Divine Order according to Melchizedek that corresponds absolutely to the Divine Orders and permeates with its Spiritual Energism All Expression and reaches the human spirit-souls that he created in his image and likeness and that have the great privilege of Direct Communion with Him, through Jesus Christ ("I and the Father are one", "You are my brothers, what I do you can do as well"), provided they are prepared to regain spiritual sight. They will abandon the interests of the temporary in order to find the Unchangeable and Eternal Divine interests.

He managed to convert all that is resplendent and of higher Meaning, Value, Virtue and Knowledge; the Hyper-laws and Permanent Immovable, Invisible Channels of an Indivisible flow of LOVE that contain both the Creator and the Creatures into a Uniquely Full and Pure way of conveying them to the expectantly anxious human Logic so that it could grasp –as much as possible - the Divine Acts.

At the same time, he tried and, in our opinion he succeeded to a large degree, if not in an unprecedented way, in conveying Elements of the Divine Truth and of the Esodimensions in oral and particularly in extremely simple written language, to the common experience of everyone concerned, so that they may be informed in every detail about who they are, where they come from, where they are going, what their role on Earth is, what their destination is, what their true origin is, how to recognize it truly, what the means that they must use are and how they will be helped in redefining Their Being and their repatriation... in relation with the Divine BEING...

Certainly, during these 30 days, he would occasionally

return to physical consciousness for a short period to fulfill the most basic needs of his body and he would tirelessly write His Apocalypse, His work *The Birth and Death of the Worlds and the Beings (matter-antimatter-hypermatter, universe-antiuniverse- hyperuniverse)* and then he would leave again...

Such Hyperevents of Outstanding human Beings, who apparently have a Special Divine Mission, who emerge into a TOTAL and EXTENSIVE ENLIGHTENMENT-THEOSIS, who even manage to BRING IT DOWN TO EARTH in an Unrivalled and Pure way using the Contemporary and Absolutely Comprehensible Word, appear very rarely, especially nowadays, and Summon-Invite us to Take Heed and to study scholastically and critically everything they bear witness to.

For this reason, it is wise for us to approach Their Works with healthy-pure critical thought and especially with great Respect, Humility and Sincerity.

SUMMARY OF MASTER N. MARGIORI'S WORK:

The Birth and Death of the Worlds and the Beings

(matter-antimatter-hypermatter, universe-antiuniverse- hyperuniverse)

So as to inform whoever is interested in *"Margiori's Apocalypse"* we quote the brief summary and the contents of his book *The Birth and Death of the Worlds and the Beings (matter-antimatter-hypermatter, universe – anti-universe - hyperuniverse)* in which he "exhausts" within all possible human limits, for the FIRST TIME on our Planet, the Greatest Topic of all Times and Peoples of the Earth, the Eschatological issue, conveying Whole Parts of the Transcendental Divine Truth (of the Divine Plan) to our Dimension and to our three-dimensional reasoning.

The Birth and Death of the Worlds and the Beings (matter-antimatter-hypermatter, universe-antiuniverse- hyperuniverse) is the tenth of the approximately 189 books of Nikolaos A. Margioris, with the first edition in 1979 and the second edition in 1990, with complementary and explanatory material.

In this work, the author gives a completely Personal answer to the Great matter of all Times, the COSMOGON-IC-ONTOGONIC and the ESCHATOLOGICAL MATTER. His mystical soul reveals its Deep Experiences and tries to give the Answer, using the Mind and the pen as a means for the hyperintellectual and the hyperconscious events. Based on these, an Eternal Creative Circle unfolds, one that is Coordinated and Created by the WORD that in our human language is called Jesus Christ.

In the said transcendental work, a Deep and Endless series of Visions prevails, combined and reinforced by Nuclear Physics, Astronomy, Astrosophy, Theology and Esoteric Philosophy, starting from the preface and arriving at the epilogue in all its immensity, offering the surprised reader some scenes of Hyper-biblical and Improbable Images.

The Birth and Death of the Worlds and the Beings (matter-antimatter-hypermatter, universe-antiuniverse-hyperuniverse) unfolds in the physical screen before the reader who follows and sees that none of the beings that are born in the various worlds of Creation are exempt or escape the Eternal Laws that determine and direct their beginning and their end.

Matter, Antimatter and Hypermatter faithfully obey and follow the executed Plan of Him, whose purpose is the Evolution of the worlds and of the beings, the products of His Essence. An endless struggle of His divided Powers bears life and form to His infinite worlds and guides the eternal BEING. This Superb and Eternal Phase during which the First sperms of Omnicreation move, is described, interpreted and depicted elaborately on the pages of this unique book...

CONTENTS OF *THE BIRTH AND DEATH OF THE WORLDS AND THE BEINGS (MATTER-ANTIMATTER-HYPERMATTER, UNIVERSE-ANTIUNIVERSE- HYPERUNIVERSE)*

PART ONE

PART TWO

PART THREE OF THE 2nd EDITION

CURRICULUM VITAE OF ILIAS KATSIAMPAS

Ilias L. Katsiampas was born on October 30th 1965 in Trikala of Thessaly (Greece) where he grew up and lives today. He is a graduate of Physical Education (TEFAA), he has worked as a journalist for the last twenty-two years and he is the writer and publisher of 15 philosophical works. He is married to Sofia A. Skoumi with whom he has two children, Lampros and Maria.

From a very young age, he expressed a strong esoteric interest in looking for the essence of things, the real meaning of life. He studied many philosophical systems as well as volumes of books on Esotericism of every kind, time and country until he met **Nikolaos A. Margioris**, the **Greek Master** of **Esotericism** (1913-1993), in whose spiritual work he recognized the presence of substantial Knowledge, the supreme real truth. He became his student and remained close to him from 1983 to his physical passing on May 6th 1993.

Among other things, he was taught the pure form of Raja Yoga and he was trained in numerous other esoteric fields of interest (Esoteric Philosophy, Esoteric Theology, Mysticism, Astrology-Astrosophy, Hypnotism-Orthopsychism, Scientific Spiritualism, Esoteric Therapeutics and so on) and gradually ascended the steps of his spiritual evolution.

The fiery and indomitable tendency and willingness of the writer to explore the Beyond in combination with his intensive training, apprenticeship and direct close relationship with his Master N. Margioris for almost a decade contributed decisively to his gradual formation of an integrated experiential clear perception-point of view on the whole field of Metaphysics as well as on the practices of meditation and mysticism.

On **January 18, 1992** with the full encouragement, guidance and in the presence of his Master, he inaugurated the **Omakoio of Trikala**, an educational-spiritual center, where all the **Yoga** systems (Mantram, Kriya, Raja, Karma, Jnani, Bhakti, Kundalini, Sahaja, Atmoliquefaction), **Esoteric Philosophy, Alternative** and **Esoteric Therapeutics** and generally **Esotericism** (Occultism and Mysticism) are taught to this day.

Since 1999, he has been active in the **Omakoio of Thessaloniki.**

In **July 2012**, along with his partners and students, he established the Association **"YOGA ACADEMY OF NIKOLAOS MARGIORIS-OMAKOIO"** as a tribute to his Master **N. Margioris** for a more holistic application of his philosophical and practical work.

He proclaims and highlights the paramount need for the widespread teaching of **Esotericism** (Introversion-Self Knowledge) in order to create healthy and balanced minds and a truly New Spiritual Man characterized by self-awareness, self-reliance, autonomy, an open mind, a giving disposition, free of materialistic pettiness and repressed desires, and an ability to better adapt and respond to the challenges of modern reality as well as to every future time of Humanity.

SCHOOLS IN OPERATION AT THE OMAKOIOS OF ATHENS, LAMIA AND TRIKALA

For the purpose of informing our readers, we would like to draw their attention to the existence and operation of three Genuine and Autonomous Metaphysical Schools (with an extensive didactic curriculum on Esotericism) which were created in the Greek area and inaugurated by the Master himself. They are the **Omakoio of Athens**, the **Omakoio of Lamia** and the **Omakoio of Trikala**.

We mention them because all three belong to Master Nikolaos A. Margiori's students-instructors, they were established with his full consent and at his urging while he was still alive, and they follow his own Spiritual Legacy and Teachings.

Certainly, every Omakoio always constitutes a Separate and Autonomous Entity-Spiritual School with its own Identity-History and Work and with its own Personality and Instructor.

At the same time, all of them are under the Protection of the Master but also in a Pythagorean Union **(Pythagorean Contact)** among themselves, while each takes care of and serves the individualized liberal philosophical work that it has undertaken under His command.

OMAKOIO OF ATHENS
SMARO I. KOSMAOGLOU
METAPHYSICAL STUDIES IN YOGA AND SHIATSU
ATHENS, GREECE

OMAKOIO OF LAMIA
DIMITRIS & KULA TSAPARA
METAPHYSICAL STUDIES IN YOGA AND SHIATSU
LAMIA, GREECE

OMAKOIO OF TRIKALA
ILIAS L. KATSIAMPAS
METAPHYSICAL STUDIES IN YOGA AND SHIATSU
21 KEFALLINIAS STREET
42100 TRIKALA, GREECE
TEL. & FAX: 0030-24310-75505 & MOBILE: 0030-
6974-580768

Web site: http://www.omakoio.gr
E-mails: omakoio@omakoio.gr & omakoeio@gmail.com

Recently, individual efforts are also being expended to make His Work more widely known with the operation – apart from everything else - of new branches in various parts of Greece.

Omakoio of Athens is extending its activities to Piraeus with a branch that will be under the supervision of Konstantinos Dimelis and which will start with the instruction of the Esoteric Philosophy of the Master and Kriya Yoga.

Also, a second branch is already in operation in Kerkyra (Corfu) under the direction of Ioannis Sgouros and Soula Pouliassi, where Esoteric Philosophy, Esoteric Therapeutics and Kriya Yoga are being taught.

The Omakoio of Lamia is expected to extend operations to Kallithea, in Athens.

Finally, the Omakoio of Trikala, apart from its current activities (with 8 years of continual and unhindered operation), is running for the second time in its history, a Complete Course of Instruction - theoretical and practical - of the multifarious work of the Master in Thessaloniki, with the ulterior motive of making His voice heard in the second capital and the potential future foundation of an Omakoio of Thessaloniki.

Some isolated activities are also undertaken by students of the Master in different parts of Greece, such as Komotini, Loutraki of Corinth, Mytilene, etc. where Esoteric Philosophy, Kriya Yoga and certain aspects of Esoteric Therapeutics are presented.

Trikala, Greece 1999

IN THE OMAKOIO OF TRIKALA THE FOLLOWING DEPARTMENTS ARE IN OPERATION:

A) PUBLICATION - SALES OF BOOKS
WHOLESALE - RETAIL

All the books written and published by the Metaphysicist, Master Nikolaos A. Margioris (189 books in total) are distributed through the Omakoio of Trikala, Greece. Please ask for the relevant price list. Also, ask for Ilias L. Katsiampas' (Nikolaos A. Margioris' student) book *From the Master's Mouth to the Student's Ear, with a Thorough Glossary of Sanskrit (Philosophic Dictionary, 400 Words) for the Students of Yoga.* The following books by the same author are in press a) *A Comprehensive Analytical Dictionary of Metaphysical Terms* b) *The Systems of Esoteric Therapeutics.*

B) KRIYA YOGA SCHOOL
PSYCHOSOMATIC - THERAPEUTICS

It started operation for the first time in Trikala, in January of 1992. Master of Metaphysics, Yoga and SHIATSU, N. Margioris revived and established the authentic Kriya Yoga. He brought back the genuine Kriya from obscurity and made it known again. He taught it in Greece for the first time in 1981 in the Omakoio of Athens and he wrote his first book without a Master, *Kriya Yoga - A Practical Method of Psychosomatic-Therapy.* In this School, many physical exercises are taught in combination with rhythmical breathing exercises (Pranayama) so that the Nervous and the Muscular system may become stronger, resulting in health and serenity, as well as the release of the trainee from stress and other psychological disturbances. Kriya is the only path which properly prepares the trainee for his initiation to Concentration (Raja Yoga).

C) RAJA YOGA SCHOOL
MIND ELEVATION FROM
CONSCIOUSNESS TO HYPERCONSCIOUSNESS

It was established and has been in operation in Trikala since December 5, 1991. Instruction is accompanied by Master Nikolaos Margioris' book *RAJA YOGA*. In Raja Yoga, the advanced students are trained only in intellectual exercises aiming to perfect and balance the Mind. The trainee strengthens his will and acquires a larger and clearer understanding of every matter that may occupy him, particularly in Metaphysics. Special exercises in concentration and hyperconcentration only found in Raja Yoga are executed with the purpose of ultimately and gradually reactivating the third and highest Mind function, hyperconsciousness.

Also all the Yoga systems such as Karma, Bhakti, Mantra, Jnani, Kundalini (Tantra) and so on, are taught.

D) SEMINARS OF SHIATSU - SUGGESTION - HYPNOTISM

Every year, many seminars on Therapeutics without medication based on the Japanese technique of SHIATSU (Namikoshi) are held, while at the same time the ancient Greek method of Massaging (Asklipieia-Amfiaraeia), of Finger-tapping (Nikolaos A. Margioris' method), of Sleep Therapy (suggestion, hypnotism) and others are taught.

E) SEMINARS AND SPEECHES OF ESOTERIC PHI-LOSOPHY

In these seminars, topics concerning the entire field of Esoteric Philosophy, Occultism and Mysticism, such as the other Dimensions; the Law of Free Will, of Karma and of Reincarnation; the life and work of great Sage Masters; the Body-Mind-Intellect-Soul-Spirit; the Divine Plan and the Evolution of Creation and so on, are presented.

F) ATMOLIQUEFACTION SCHOOL
SLIMMING ONLY FOR WOMEN

This department of the Omakoio of Trikala operates once or twice a year and its program lasts for about three months. Special physical exercises in combination with the proper breathing exercises (Pranayama - N. Margioris' system) are taught. These are very effective in activating the organism, resulting in perspiration and the burning of fat. At the same time, muscles are strengthened without any mechanical means or medicine.

G) ESOTERIC KEY
STUDIES THROUGH A CORRESPONDENCE COURSE
IN THE FOLLOWING BRANCHES OF ESOTERICISM

1) ASTROLOGY - ASTROSOPHY
2) ESOTERIC PHILOSOPHY
3) SCIENTIFIC SPIRITUALISM
4) HYPNOTISM - ORTHOPSYCHISM
5) ESOTERIC THERAPEUTICS
6) ESOTERIC INITIATION
7) MEDITATION
8) DESYMBOLISM

Those who would like further information and analytical prospectuses about any branch may request them from the OMAKOIO OF TRIKALA, 21 Kefallinias Str., 42100, Trikala, Greece, or call **Mr. Ilias Katsiampas** at the telephone number 0030-24310-75505 or 0030-6974-580768 (mobile).

All the books, essays, journals and correspondence courses by Master Nikolaos A. Margioris, founder of the Omakoio of Athens, are available at the Omakoio of Trikala.

BIBLIOGRAPHY OF THE BOOK

The entire Work is the result of the painstaking research, study, processing and composition of multiple elements and details that the director of the Omakoio of Trikala has managed through his sound and certified experience on Esoteric Reality.

His decade-long studies under the immediate close personal tutelage, relationship and cooperation with his Master Nikolaos A. Margioris, the well-found Esoteric Knowledge that he Composed to an incredible degree Within him, his small personal experiences and the un-interrupted contact and cooperation with his fellow students have given him the opportunity to encounter and validate on multiple occasions and levels the Esoteric Knowledge that his Master conveyed to him, especially everything that concerns the Apocalypse of John.

Foremost, however, for the present Work he used certain parts from the Pure Preserved Oral Teachings of his Master that concerned the Explanation of the Apocalypse of John (as it was presented in this book) which has been validated by the widespread Knowledge and Esoteric Theology that he gained from the exhaustive dialogues with the Master as well as from the study of ALL his works independently, especially from the books *The Birth and Death of the Worlds and the Beings (matter-antimatter-hypermatter, universe-antiuniverse-hyperuniverse), Posthumous Life* and *Esoteric Philosophy.*

Below you will find the full Bibliography that the director of the Omakoio of Trikala additionally took into consideration when composing this work.

I) PUBLISHED BOOKS
BY NIKOLAOS A. MARGIORIS
(copyrights belong to his heirs)

1. Patapios, the Humble Philosopher and Saint from Egypt, 1st edition in 1970 (156 pages), 2nd edition in 1987 (220 pages), with supplementary and explanatory material, 3rd edition in 2005 (220 pages).

2. Light in the Dark, 1st edition in 1975 (300 pages), 2nd edition in 1987 (429 pages) with supplementary and explanatory material, 3rd edition in 2005 (429 pages).

3. Theurgy Teaches the Eternal Way of the Soul, 1st edition in 1975 (318 pages), 2nd edition in 1987 (408 pages), with supplementary and explanatory material.

4. The Other View of Erich Von Daniken's Dogma, 1st edition in 1976 (318 pages), 2nd edition in 1994 (372 pages), with supplementary and explanatory material. ISBN: 960-7484-00-2.

5. The Secret of Hatha Yoga, 1st edition in 1976 (111 pages), 2nd edition in 1977 (155 pages). ISBN: 960-7484-04-5.

6. Pythagorean Arithmosophy, 1st edition in 1977 (168 pages), 2nd edition in 1987 (271 pages), 3rd edition in 1993 (276 pages) with supplementary and explanatory material, 4th edition in 2000 (276 pages), 5th edition in 2004 (282 pages). ISBN: 960-7152-06-09.

7. The Eleusinian Mysteries, 1st edition in 1978 (99 pages), 2nd edition in 1987 (159 pages), 3rd edition in 1993

(178 pages) with supplementary and explanatory material, 4th edition in 1999 (183 pages). ISBN: 960-7152-11-5.

8. The Last Day of Socrates, 1st edition in 1978 (111 pages), 2nd edition in 1988 (152 pages), with supplementary and explanatory material.

9. The Pharaohs Akhenaten and Tutankhamun, 1st edition in 1978 (151 pages), 2nd edition in 1991 (311 pages), with supplementary and explanatory material. ISBN: 960-7152-00-X.

10. The Birth and Death of the Worlds and the Beings (matter-antimatter-hypermatter, universe-antiuniverse- hyperuniverse), 1st edition in 1979 (195 pages), 2nd edition in 1990 (p 323 pages), with supplementary and explanatory material, 3nd edition in 2009 (323 pages). ISBN: 960-85024-5-4.

11. Dravidians, the Ancestors of the Greeks (Synopsis) in English, 1st edition in 1979 (45 pages).

12. The Reign of Minos, the Great King of Crete, 1st edition in 1979 (88 pages), 2nd edition in 1997 (105 pages). ISBN: 960-7484-06-1.

13. Dravidians, the Ancestors of Greeks, 1st edition in 1979 (88 pages), 2nd edition in 1989 (143 pages), with supplementary and explanatory material, 3rd edition in 1996 (167 pages), 4th edition in 2004 (166 pages).

14. Eastern and Western White and Black Magic, 1st edition in 1979 (134 pages),

15. White Magic, 2nd edition in 1992 (227 pages) with

supplementary and explanatory material. ISBN: 960-7152-03-4.

16. Barefoot They Dance on Fire (Anastenaria), 1st edition in 1980 (95 pages).

17. Posthumous Life, 1st edition in 1982 (256 pages), 2nd edition in 1993 (262 pages), 3rd edition in 2010 (262 pages). ISBN: 960-7152-09-3.

18. Raja Yoga, 1st edition in 1983 (208 pages).

19. The Two-Volume Metaphysical Encyclopaedia, 1st edition in 1985/86 (Volume A, 443 pages, Volume B, 752 pages).

20. Kriya Yoga – A Practical Method of Psychosomatic Therapy, 1st edition in 1988 (357 pages), 2nd edition in 2000 (359 pages).

21. The Desymbolism of Greek Mythology, 1st edition in 1988 (521 pages), 2nd edition in 2002 (562 pages).

22. The Three-Dimensional and Four-Dimensional World, 1st edition in 1989 (214 pages), 2nd edition in 2007 (222 pages). ISBN: 960-85024-3-8.

23. Mystical Teachings, Volume A, 1st edition in 1991 (346 pages). ISBN: 960-85024-1-1 SET 960-85024-7-0.

24. Karma. The Law of Retributive Justice, 1st edition in 1989 (373 pages), 2nd edition in 1996 (373 pages), 3rd edition in 2009 (373 pages). ISBN: 960-85024-0-3.

25. Reincarnation, 1st edition in 1990 (286 pages), 2nd edition in 2009 (286 pages). ISBN: 960-85024-4-6.

26. The Chiroplastic Therapeutics of SHIATSU, Volume A, 1st edition in 1990 (533 pages). ISBN: 960-85024-6-2.

27. Psychotherapeutics without Medication, 1st edition in 1991 (325 pages). ISBN: 960-85024-8-9.

28. Mysticism. Christocentric and Christocratic Mysticism, 1st edition in 1991 (331 pages). ISBN: 960-85024-9-7.

29. Occultism (Occultology), Volume A, 1st edition in 1991 (391 pages). ISBN: 960-7152-01-8, 960-7152-02-6.

30. Occultism (Occultology), Volume B, 1st edition in 1992 (428 pages). ISBN: 960-7152-01-8, T.2. 960-7152-04-2.

31. The Chiroplastic Therapeutics of SHIATSU, Volume B, 1st edition in 1993 (395 pages). ISBN: SET 960-7152-07-7, 960-7152-08-5.

32. Mystical Teachings, Volume B, 1st edition in 1993 (388 pages). ISBN: SET 960-85024-7-0, 960-7152-05-0.

33. Mystical Teachings, Volume C, 1st edition in 1994 (379 pages). ISBN: SET 960-85024-7-0, 960-7152-10-7.

34. The Chiroplastic Therapeutics of SHIATSU, Volume C, 1st edition in 1993 (255 pages).

35. Occultism (Occultology), Volume C, 1st edition in 1997, 103 pages. ISBN: 960-7484-05-3.

II) ESSAYS BY NIKOLAOS. A. MARGIORIS

1. SCHOOL OF ASKLEPIANS - HYPNOTHERAPISTS

2. CARL VON REICHENBACH

3. SCHOOL OF AESKLEPIANS- SPIRITUAL THERAPISTS THEOPHRASTUS PARACELSUS

4. MAGNETOTHERAPY

5. ASKLEPIAIA AND AMFIARAEIA

6. THE THERAPY FROM BEFORE TIME

7. THE CELL AND LIFE MYSTERY

8. ECTOPLASM

9. ESSENES

10. APPARITIONS OF IDOLS OF LIVING PEOPLE

11. ANASTENARIA

12. CREATION OF THE WORLDS

13. MYSTICISM

14. DRAVIDIANS, THE FIRST GREEKS OF THE AEGEAN SEA

15. THE CONTROL OF VIBRATIONS

16. WHAT IS ESOTERICISM?

17. THE HOLY SCROLLS OF THE ESSENE RULES

18. EROS AND LOVE

19. PROPER NUTRITION, PROPER DIET, WEIGHT LOSS

20. THERAPEUTICS WITHOUT MEDICATION

21. THERAPEUTICS THROUGH HYPNOTISM

22. THERAPY OF PSYCHOPATHY

23. SHIATSU. THERAPEUTIC METHOD TWO VOLUMES (1st seminar)

24. SHIATSU. THERAPEUTIC METHOD TWO VOLUMES (2nd seminar)

25. SHIATSU. THERAPEUTUC METHOD TWO VOLUMES (3rd seminar)

26. SHIATSU. THERAPEUTIC METHOD TWO VOLUMES (4th seminar)

27. SHIATSU. THERAPEUTIC METHOD TWO VOLUMES (5th seminar)

28. SHIATSU. THERAPEUTIC METHOD ONE VOLUME (6th seminar)

29. SHIATSU. THERAPEUTIC METHOD ONE VOLUME (7th seminar)

30. SHIATSU. THERAPEUTIC METHOD ONE VOLUME (8th seminar)

31. SHIATSU. THERAPEUTIC METHOD ONE VOLUME (9th seminar)

32. SHIATSU. THERAPEUTIC METHOD ONE VOLUME (10th seminar)

33. SHIATSU. THERAPEUTIC METHOD ONE VOLUME (11th seminar)

III) OMAKOIO JOURNAL
BY NIKOLAOS A. MARGIORIS (49 issues)

The best **metaphysical** *and* **occultist magazine** of our country. **Its every article** *is a* **revelation. Its every page** is an **enlightenment.** It contains **well-documented** *and* **rare metaphysical analyses** on plenty of esoteric matters. It comes in hexads. It was in circulation for **8 years (1977-1985)** in bimonthly publications. The first issue is number 2 and the last is number 49 (total of pages: 1658). There are 8 hexads at **25.00€** per hexad.

IV) ESOTERIC KEY
BY NIKOLAOS A. MARGIORIS

Esotericism and **Metaphysics** are presented in complete form in their practical application and they give the student the **KEY OF KNOWLEDGE.**

Seven Branches *of* **Esotericism**, with **thirty** or **thirty-three** treatises of lessons. Every Branch contains approximately ten or eleven triads or thirty to thirty-three chapters – lessons. See summaries and contents for every branch separately in our site: www.omakoio.gr

Every lesson – triad costs **15.00 Euro. Enrolment** is a one-time fee of **10.00 Euro.** Ask for informative printed enrolment forms for the Esoteric Key branches of study by correspondence course.

The Branches are the following:

1) MEDITATION
2) HYPNOTISM - ORTHOPSYCHISM
3) SCIENTIFIC SPIRITUALISM

4) ESOTERIC PHILOSOPHY
5) ESOTERIC INITIATION
6) ASTROLOGY - ASTROSOPHY
7) ESOTERIC THERAPEUTICS
8) DESYMBOLISM

Nikolaos Margiori's books that are translated into English, or that are currently in the process of being translated, are the following:

1) Dravidians, the Ancestors of the Greeks (translated, in a book), **2) Posthumous Life** (translated), **3) Birth and Death of the Worlds and of Beings** (matter, antimatter, hypermatter, universe, antiuniverse, hyperuniverse) (in the process of being translated), **4) Kriya Yoga** (translated) and **5) Raja Yoga** (translated).

BOOKS BY ILIAS L. KATSIAMPAS (N. MARGIORIS' STUDENT) OMAKOIOS OF TRIKALA AND OF THESSALONIKI, GREECE (AND YOGA ACADEMY OF NIKOLAOS MARGIORIS – OMAKOIO)

My own books (**Ilias Katsiampas**, student of **Master N. Margioris**) that relate directly to Margioris' work, translated into English, are the following:

1) 10-year Anniversary of the Establishment of the Omakoio of Athens by Master N. A. Margioris. A bilingual **Greek-English 1999 edition** in an A4 thermalbound edition, the Greek text consisting of 34 pages and the English text of 33 pages.

2) A Full and Most Analytical Dictionary – Guide of Metaphysical Meanings, in press.

3) Asklepian Art and the Systems of Esoteric Therapeutics, in press.

4) Bilingual Greek-English Magazine "New Omakoio", size A4, 1st issue, of 100 pages. All the 189 writings of Master Nikolaos Margioris are included in Greek and in English, with a photo of the cover, summaries and contents for each one separately, esoteric articles and the Schools-Omakoios that function in Greece.

5) Collection Articles – Advice & Interviews of Ilias L. Katsiampas, 1st edition in an A4 thermal-bound edition. October 2004. First Reward from the International Union (Company) Greek Man of letters (DEEL).

6) **Esoteric and Spiritual Experiences of Master Nikolaos A. Margioris.** A bilingual **Greek-English edition** in an A4 thermal-bound edition. 1st edition 2004.

7) **From Deep Metaphysical Correspondence.** In Greek, 1st edition 2007, 400 pages.

8) **From the Master's Mouth to the Student's Ear, with a thorough glossary of Sanskrit (philosophic dictionary, 400 words) for the students of Yoga**, 1st edition 1995 (270 pages), dimension 24X17, ISBN: 960-85735-0-5. In the Greek language, it is available in book form. The English translation is also available in an A4 thermal-bound edition.

9) **Handbook – Guide for Staff and Instructors of Esotericism According to Master Nikolaos A. Margioris' Work.** It exists **in Greek** in an A4 thermal-bound edition (202 pages), 1st edition 2003 and **in English** as a separate edition (206 pages), **only for the members of the Omakoios.**

10) **Inauguration of the Omakoio of Lamia by Master N. A. Margioris.** A bilingual **Greek-English 2000 edition** in an A4 thermal-bound edition, the Greek text consisting of 36 pages and the English text of 22 pages.

11) **Inauguration of the Omakoio of Trikala by Master N. A. Margioris.** A bilingual **Greek-English 1999 edition** in an A4 thermal-bound edition, the Greek text consisting of 57 pages and the English text of 38 pages.

12) **Meditation and Mysticism, Raja and Kundalini Yoga (Theory and practice)**, in press.

13) Plagues and Provocations of our Time. The Metaphysical View. In press.

14) Prayer Book and Poems of Master Nikolaos A. Margioris. A bilingual **Greek-English edition.** In book form. 1ˢᵗ edition 2004. First Reward from the International Union (Company) Greek Man of letters (DEEL).

15) The Apocalypse of John as Explained by Master Nikolaos A. Margioris (A bilingual Greek-English edition, supervised and with extensive analytical annotations by his student, Ilias L. Katsiampas), 1ˢᵗ edition 1999, ISBN: 960-85735-1-3. Second Award from the International Union (Company) Greek Man of letters (DEEL).

16) The Mystery of Death and the Posthumous Course of the Soul. In press.

17) The Question of Aliens. In press.

Information

Ilias Katsiampas
21 Kefallinias str., 42100 Trikala, Greece
Tel. and Fax 0030-24310-75505
or mobile: 0030-6974-580768

Website: http://www.omakoio.gr
or https://omakoio.blogspot.com

E-mails: omakoio@omakoio.gr or omakoeio@gmail.com

PRESENTATIONS ON YOUTUBE AND ON FACEBOOK
OF THE 189 WRITINGS
OF THE MODERN GREEK MYSTIC, NIKOLAOS A.
MARGIORIS (1913-1993)
AND OF 15 BOOKS BY HIS STUDENT, ILIAS KAT-
SIAMPAS

IN ENGLISH

VIDEO PRESENTATION IN ENGLISH OF 35 BOOKS OF
MODERN GREEK MYSTIC, NIKOLAOS A. MARGIORIS
(1913-1993). With subtitles in English.

DURATION: 61 MINUTES.

The video was posted at http://youtu.be/GUbJ3RbhpIQ

https://www.youtube.com/watch?v=GUbJ3RbhpIQ&featu
re=youtu.be

VIDEO (PRIVATE) OF THE INAUGURATION OF
THE NEOPYTHAGOREAN SCHOOL - OMAKOIO OF
TRIKALA BY GREEK SPIRITUAL MASTER NIKO-
LAOS A. MARGIORIS THAT TOOK PLACE ON SAT-
URDAY, JANUARY 18th 1992, 8:00 p.m. With sub-
titles in English.

Part A of VIDEO (Duration: 2:02:44)

http://youtu.be/KU3JalIc5HI or

https://www.youtube.com/watch?v=KU3JalIc5HI&feature
=youtu.be

VIDEO (PRIVATE) OF THE INAUGURATION OF THE NEOPYTHAGOREAN SCHOOL-OMAKOIO OF TRIKALA BY GREEK SPIRITUAL MASTER NIKOLAOS A. MARGIORIS THAT TOOK PLACE ON SATURDAY, JANUARY 19th 1992, 8:00 p.m. With subtitles in English.

Part B of VIDEO (Duration: 1:26:15)

http://youtu.be/YR3I-WqVawI or

https://www.youtube.com/watch?v=YR3I-WqVawI&feature=youtu.be

VIDEO (PRIVATE) of the Celebration of the 10 Years Since the Foundation of the Omakoio of Athens by Master Nikolaos A. Margioris.

Friday, Nov. 27, 1987, 21:00 AND

Banquet and Speech at the Golden Age Hotel, Athens, with an Award of Honorary Medals by Master Nikolaos A. Margioris to his students.

July 1989

Video Duration: 2h & 7min

http://youtu.be/D79MIXeDgaE

https://www.youtube.com/watch?v=D79MIXeDgaE&feature=youtu.be

Produced and translated into English by Ilias Katsiampas

BOOKS BY OTHER WRITERS
RECOMMENDED FOR STUDY

- *ABOUT THE CONTINUAL HOLY COMMUNION of the sacraments of CHRIST*, by Nikodemus of the Holy Mountain, Nektarios Panagopoulos Editions.

- *ADVISORY MANUAL*, by Nikodemus of the Holy Mountain, Nektarios Panagopoulos Editions

- ALSO THE WORKS OF PYTHAGORAS - PLATO - SOCRATES - PLOTINUS - HERAKLEITOS - HESIOD - PLUTARCHUS - ORPHISM - GREEK MYTHOLOGY etc.

- THE HYMN BOOK OF THE ORTHODOX CHURCH.

- *ANTONIOS THE GREAT*, Vas. Rigopoulos editions.

- *ATHENAGORAS THE ECUMENICAL TO THE NEW IDEAS*, by Professor D. Tsakonas (D. Tsakonas editions).

- *AUTOBIOGRAPHY OF A YOGI*, by Paramhansa Yogananda, Estia Bookshop.

- *BHAGAVAD GITA*, by Demetrios Galanos, Dodoni Editions. By Thodoros Pantouvas, Kardamitsa Editions and by Tim. T. Vratsanos, Bookshop of Estia Editions.

- *GREEKS AND INDIANS (TWO WORLDS MEET EACH OTHER)*, by Dimitris K. Velissaropoulos, Dodoni Editions.

- HINDU PHILOSOPHY, by Helmut Bernard, Konidiaris Editions.

- *HISTORY OF INDIAN PHILOSOPHY*, by Dimitris K. Velissaropoulos, Dodoni Editions.

- *INTERPRETATIVE DICTIONARY OF INDIAN PHILOSOPHY*, by Theodoros Pantouvas.

- *INTRODUCTION TO SATHYA SAI BABA'S TEACHING*, Harmonious Life Editions.

- *JNANA YOGA*, by Swami Vivekananda, Konidiaris Editions.

- *KENA AND OTHER UPANISHADS*, by Sri Aurobindo, New Times Editions.

- *LIBRARY OF THE GREEK FATHERS, ADAMANTIOS ORIGHENIS*, Edition of the Apostolic Deaconship of the Church of Greece.

- *LITURGY, THE RITUALS IN THE CHURCH*, by Mich. K. Papadopoulos, Prince Notarios of the Ecumenical Throne, Eptalofos Editions, A.B.E.E.

- *ON BASIC HUMAN RIGHTS*,   Bhagwan Shree Rajnees.

- *ORIGHENI'S THEOLOGICAL AND PHILOSOPHICAL SYSTEM*, by Professor John Ant. Kaldelis, Mytilene, 1978.

- *PANHELLENIC SYMPOSIUM THEOFILOS KAIRIS* (Center for Neo-Hellenic Studies), Gutenberg Editions.

- *PARAHAMSA SATYANANDA'S TEACHINGS*, Satyananda Ashram of Greece.

- *PLATO AND UPANISHADS*, Vassilis Vitsaxis, Bookshop of the Estia Editions.

- *PREDICTIONS IN THE THEOLOGY OF THE UNBUILT*

ACTS (STUDY OF SAINT GREGORIOS PALAMAS), by Stavros Giagazoglou, Tertios Editions, Katerini).

- *PURANAS, INDIAN MYTHOLOGY AND TRADITION*, by Irini A. Panaghiotidou, Tassos Pitsilas Editions.

- *RAMAKRISHNA, THE DEMIGOD, VIVEKANANDA THE WISE*, by Romain Rolland, Divry's Editions.

- *RAMAKRISHNA, THE MADMAN OF GOD*, Spiritual Sun Editions.

- *RAMAYANA, THE FIRST GREAT EPIC OF INDIA* (K. Stefanidi's translation), by Valmiki, New Age Library.

- *SAINT GREGORIOS PALAMAS*, Thessaloniki Editions.

- *SPIRITUAL EXERCISES*, by Nikodemus of the Holy Mountain, Nektarios Panagopoulos Editions.

- *SRI RAMAKRISHNA 'S GOSPEL*, Konidiaris Editions.

- *TALES FROM INDIA*, Apopira Editions.

- *THE AESTHETICS OF THE HOLY SOBER FATHERS*, 5 Volumes, "The Garden of Virgin Mary" Editions

- *THE ASCETICS OF LOVE*, by Sister Gabriel the Elderly, Eptalofos ABEE Editions.

- *THE FALSE INSCRIPTIONS OF DIONYSIUS THE AREOPAGITE* ("About the Ecclesiastical and Heavenly Hierarchy", "About Divine Names and Mystical Theology", "Theological Formulations and Symbolical Theology").

According to Master Nikolaos A. Margioris, the monk Saint Patapios - his holy relics are preserved in his Monastery, at

Loutraki of Corinth - is the one who wrote Dionysius the Areopagite's false-inscriptions and due to his great humbleness, he put the name of the first Bishop of Athens in the place of his own name, which was common practice in those times. Anyone interested may find some details in the Master's book *Patapios, the Humble Philosopher and Saint from Egypt.*

- *THE FUNDAMENDAL PHILOSOPHIES OF INDIA* (The six classic systems with the Kashmir Shaivism), Theos Bernard, Konidiaris Editions.

- *THE GERONTIKON, MAXIMS OF ELDERLY SAINTS*, The Orthodox Institution Apostle Varnavas Editions.

- *THE GREAT INITIATES*, by Edward Schure, Cactus Editions.

- *THE INVISIBLE WAR*, by Nikodemus of the Holy Mountain, Tinos Editions.

- *THE LADDER OF JOHN THE SINAITE*, The Parakletos Holy Monastery Editions.

- *THE LIGHT OF THE SOUL*, by Alice Bailey, Luicis Trust editions.

- *THE NEW TESTAMENT* - THE ORIGINAL TEXT TRANSLATED IN THE DEMOTIC LANGUAGE, Bible Society Editions

- *THE NEW TESTAMENT WITH A BRIEF INTERPRETATION*, by Pan. N. Trempelas, Theologians' Editions "The Saviour"

- *THE OCCULTIST EVOLUTION OF HUMANITY*, by Jinarajadasa, Theosophical Publishing House.

- *THE OLD TESTAMENT*

- *THE SECRET DOCTRINE*, by Helena Petrovna Blavatsky, Five Volumes, Spiritual Sun Editions.

- *THE SYSTEMS OF YOGA*, by Kirpal Singh.

- *THE TEACHINGS OF SRI RAMANA MAHARSHI*, by David Godman, Eternal Charioteer Editions.

- *THE TEN BASIC UPANISHADS*, Iamvlichos Editions.

- *THE UNIVERSING KNOWLEDGE*, by Jan van Rijckenborgh - Catharose de Petri, Lectorium Rosicrucianum.

- *THE VALLEY OF THE ROSES* (by Paul Amadeus Dienach), Arrangement, Criticism, Analysis, Comments by Julie Pitsouli, Kritonou Editions.

- *THE VALLEY OF THE ROSES*, by Paul Amadeus Dienach, Vakon editions.

- *THE WHEEL*, by Nikodemus of the Holy Mountain, Vas. Rigopoulos Editions.

- *THOUGHT AND FAITH*, two volumes, by Vassilis Vitsaxis, Bookshop of Estia Editions.

- *UPANISHADS*, by Jean Varenne, Dodoni Editions.

- *YOGA*, by Mircea Eliade, I. Chatzinikolis Editions.

- *YOGA*, Swami Vivekananda (Raja, Bhakti, Karma and Patanjali's aphorisms, with Vivekananda's comments), Divry's Editions or/and Konidiaris Editions.

GREEK WRITERS WHO USED EXCERPTS FROM THE 189 WORKS OF THE AUTHOR AND THE MODERN METAPHYSICAL MASTER NIKOLAOS A. MARGIORIS (AND CITED IT IN THEIR BIBLIOGRAPHY)

(Search and classification by his student
Ilias L. Katsiampas)

1) *THE DECIPHERING OF THE PHAISTOS DISC - GENESIS THE GREEK SPIRIT DESCENDED FROM SIRIUS* by Thodoros Axiotis, editions Smyrniotakis. It refers to N.A. Margiori's book *Eleusinian Mysteries.*

2) *SEARCHING FOR THE LOST ARK,* by Thodoros Axiotis. Smirniotakis Editions. It refers to the book *Eleusinian Mysteries* by N.A. Margioris.

3) *ARGO - THE FIRST ARGONAUTIC EXPEDITION OF 3.500 B.C.* by Thodoros Axiotis, Smirniotakis Editions. It refers to the book *Eleusinian Mysteries* by N.A. Margioris.

4) *THE CRETAN MYSTERIES,* by George Siettos. Pyrinos Kosmos, Athens 1995 editions. It refers to the book *Light in the Dark,* by N.A. Margioris.

5) *ANCIENT SURVIVALS IN CHRISTIANITY* by Georgios Siettos, Altebaran Editions, Athens 1994. It refers to N.A. Margiori's book *Light in the Dark,* 1975 edition.

6) *THE PYTHAGOREAN MYSTERIES* by Georgios Siettos. Pyrinos Kosmos Editions, Athens 1933. It refers to N.A. Margiori's book *Light in the Dark,* 1975 edition.

7) *PYTHAGORA'S SECRET CODE AND THE DECI-PHERING OF HIS TEACHINGS*, by Ippokratis Dako-glou, New Thesis editions, 1st , 2nd, 3rd Volumes. It refers to N.A. Margiori's books *The Two-Volume Metaphysical Encyclopaedia, Theurgy Teaches the Eternal Way of the Soul* and *Pythagorean Arithmosophy*.

8) *EGYPT YESTERDAY AND TODAY*, by Paraskevi Vlahogianni, Protovoulia Editions, Athens 1992. It refers to N.A. Margiori's books *Pythagorean Arithmosophy* and *The Pharaohs*.

9) "PYRAMIS' by Paul Varouchakis. Pyrinos Kosmos Editions, Athens 1992. It refers to N.A. Margiori's books *The Three-Dimensional and Four-Dimensional World, The Birth and Death of the Worlds and the Beings (mat-ter-antimatter-hypermatter, universe-antiuniverse- hy-peruniverse), Pythagorean Arithmosophy* and *The Pha-raohs* of N. A. Margioris.

10) *THE BASIC PRINCIPLES OF METAPSYCHICS* by Aspasia Papadomichelaki, Center of Metaphysical Infor-mation Editions, Athens 1992. It refers to the books *What is Esotericism, Pythagorean Arithmosophy, The Essenes, The Pharaohs, The Eleusinian Mysteries, The Birth and Death of the Worlds and the Beings (matter-antimatter-hypermatter, universe-antiuniverse- hyperuniverse), The Three-Dimensional and Four-Dimensional World, The Control of Vibrations, Esoteric Philosophy* and *Posthu-mous Life*.

11) *THE MAGICAL WORK*, by Aspasia Papadomichela-ki, Athens 1993. It refers to N.A. Margiori's book *Eastern and Western White and Black Magic*, **1st Edition, 1980**".

12) *FIREWALKING AND ANASTENARIDES*, by Iassonas Evaghelou, Dodoni Editions. 4th Edition Athens 1994. It refers to N.A. Margiori's book *Walking on Fire - Anastenaria* and to his point of view about Anastenaria.

13) *THE TRUTH ABOUT PREHISTORY, HISTORY AND THE GREEK CIVILIZATION – VOLUME A* by Marinos Razis, Montreal, Quebec, Canada, 1995. It refers to N.A. Margiori's books *The Desymbolism of the Greek Mythology* and *Dravidians, the Ancestors of Greeks.*

14) THE TRUTH ABOUT PREHISTORY, HISTORY AND THE GREEK CIVILIZATION – VOLUME B, by Marinos Razis, Montreal, Quebec, Canada 1997. It refers to the books *The Desymbolism of Greek Mythology, The Two-Volume Metaphysical Encyclopaedia, The Reign of Minos, the Great King of Crete, The Eleusinian Mysteries, Dravidians, the Ancestors of the Greeks*, of N.A. Margioris and to **Ilias Katsiampa's book** *From the Master's Mouth to the Student's Ear.*

15) ON THE PATH OF SELF-KNOWLEDGE (issues about the soul) by Aristidis N. Oihaliotis, Athens 1985. It refers to N.A. Margiori's books *Pythagorean Arithmosophy* and *Dravidians, the First Greeks of the Aegean Sea".*

16) *SAINT PATAPIOS*, by Styl. Papadopoulos, professor at the University of Athens, 1995, The Hermits of the Holy Monastery of Saint Patapios Editions. It refers to N.A. Margiori's book *The Birth and Death of the Worlds and the Beings (matter-antimatter-hypermatter, universe-antiuniverse- hyperuniverse).*

17) *MONISM (Physical Sciences and Philosophy)* by Iassonas Evaghelou, Savvalas Editions, 2nd edition, Athens

1996. It refers to Nikolaos A. Magriori's book *The Birth and Death of the Worlds and the Beings (matter-antimatter-hypermatter, universe-antiuniverse- hyperuniverse)*.

18) *THE PHAISTOS DISC SPEAKS GREEK* by Efi Polighiannaki, Georgiadis Editions, Athens, 1996. It refers to Nikolaos Margiori's English book **Dravidians, the Pre-Hellenic Greeks**.

19) *THE ANCIENT GREEK PANKRATION ATHLETIC EVENT, THE TRUTH ABOUT MARTIAL ARTS - THE FIGHTING ARTS*, by Lazaros E. Savidhis, 1997 edition. It refers to Nikolaos A. Margiori's books **Dravidians, the Ancestors of the Greeks** and *The Reign of Minos, the Great King of Crete*.

20) *THE DELUGE OF DEUCALION*, by Georgios K. Atsalis, 1st edition 1986, 2nd edition 1993, Nea Thesis. It refers to the book *Dravidians, the Ancestors of the Greeks* by Nikolaos A. Margioris

21) *ASTROBIOCHEMICAL MEDECINE. THE SCIENCE FROM THE PAST, THERAPY OF THE FUTURE*, by Michalis P. Rodopoulos, 1st edition April 1993. It refers to N. Margiori's book *The Three-Dimensional and Four-Dimensional World*.

22) *THE HIDDEN TRUTHS. AN ESOTERIC TREATISE. PLANET EARTH - PART 1*, by Michalis P. Rodopoulos, 1st edition in September 1997. It refers to the illustration of Hydra on the cover of N. Margiori's book under the title *Psychotherapeutics without medicines*, as well as to the internal cover of the book *Posthumous Life*.

23) *PLANET EARTH, ZERO TIME, GREEK SURVIVE, VOLUME C*, by Michalis P. Rodopoulos. It dedicates a

whole chapter to Margiori's point of view about the Dravidians, as well as to other references concerning Margiori's esoteric point of view.

24) *ELEUSINIAN MYSTERIES* by Anestis Keramidas, Istoriognosia Editions. There is a reference to the book *Eleusinian Mysteries* by N. A. Margioris.

25) *THE FOREKNOWLEDGE OF THE DELPHI*, by Ioannis Fourakis. It mentions Chattergi's and Margioris' view that the Dravidians are the ancestors of the Greek people who lived in the wider area of the Mediterranean basin.

26) *THE TETRACTYS OF IONIA AND THE IONIAN LANGUAGE*, *by* Nikolaos Andreadakis, Georgiadi Editions, Athens: 1999.

27) *THE TABOU OF ENLIGHTENMENT by* Eleni Ierodiakonou, Esoptron Editions, Athens: 2008. In Ch. 7 (In Search of a Master) she makes extensive reference to her meeting and her profoundly positive experience with N.A. Margioris.

28) *THE UNSEEN ASPECT OF THE INDOEUROPEAN ISSUE (THE THEORY OF THE SUBMERGED AEGAEIS)*, by Kostas Skandalis, Georgiadi Editions. It mentions N. A. Margioris' book *Dravidians, the Ancestors of the Greeks.*

29) *VIOLET FLAME, PRACTICAL THERAPEUTICS*, by Nitsele-Eleni Grammatakakis, Andromeda Editions, 2009. The article of N. Margioris about St. Germain or Master Rakoczi, which has been taken from the magazine 'Omakoio' (49 issues in total), is included unabridged in the last chapter of the book (i.e.: the 14th)

30) *PANEGYPTIA* MAGAZINE: A periodic publication of the Egyptiot Greek Association, 25th Year, issue no 147, May-June 2009. N. Nikitaridis' extensive feature article about the character and work of Nikolaos Margioris, as an Egyptiot Greek, and especially about Margioris receiving 60th place among the 100 Greatest Greeks that ever lived. The information for this feature article was taken from the following sources: www.omakoio.gr [18-6-2001] – masonic publications – 'Trito Mati' Magazine, issue 28 [9/1993] and 35 [5/1994].

31) *YOGA, A PHILOSOPHY OF LIFE*, Porfyra Editions, Ed. Sophia Digeni.

It mentions the books *Kriya Yoga* and *Raja Yoga* of Master Nikolaos Margioris, and includes a significant amount of information taken from them, as well as the method of Atmoliquefaction- Weight Loss and Detoxification, which N. Margioris used and taught. His students use it to this day.

32) *IOANNIS A. KAPODISTRIAS, THE SAINT OF POLITICS (THE PAST AND THE PRESENT BASED ON HIS UNPUBLISHED LETTERS)*, by Ioannis S. Kornilakis, Elaia Editions. The book by N. Margioris *Pythagorean Arithmosophy* is mentioned among the books that the author consulted.

33) *HISTORY OF THE FOUNDATION OF THE OSIRIS LODGE No. 117, IN EAST ATHENS. SIXTY YEARS OF BROTHER STAMATI VAZAKOPOULOS' MASONIC JOURNEY. ALSO THE SACRED PARTHENON LODGE, No. 376, EAST ALEXANDRIA*, by Stamatis Vazakopoulos, Athina Editions, 2010.

The book was sent as a complimentary gift to Ilias Katsiampas with the following dedication: 'To the Beloved spiritual child of my co-founder of the Sacred Osiris Lodge, No 117, in East Athens, and first Reverend Brother NIKOLAOS MARGIORIS, and his companion in this spiritual cultivation, ILIAS KATSIAMPAS with immense appreciation and admiration for his Work. The Dean: Stamatis Vazakopoulos, 14/5/2010.'

In this book there are four main references to N. Margioris.

34) *ASTROLOGY. THE WORDS OF THE STARS* . Written by Lilian Simou.1st Edition, 2006. Dimeli Editions. The work of N. Margioris *Astrology-Astrosophy* is mentioned in the book's bibliography.

35) EVAGEIS EN TI KAMINO, (CHARITABLES IN THE FURNACE) A DOCUMENTARY ABOUT THE ANASTENARIA It was broadcast by ET-3. Production-Direction: Ilias Iosifidis, Zopyros Editions. There is a reference to the book of Nikolaos Margioris *Walking on Fire – Anastenaria*.

36) *GOD AND MAN. PHILOSOPHICAL VIEWS.* Olistikis Armonias Editions. It contains the philosophical views of 16 columnists. Two of them mention Nikolaos Margioris and his work.

37) *COSMOGENESIS: ACCORDING TO THE MEMORY OF NATURE*, KIVELI EDITIONS. The author Kostas Ollandezos is a student of N. Margioris.

The above mentioned books are just some of the few that have come to the attention of Ilias Katsiampas (Manager

of the OMAKOIO Yoga School in Trikala and Thessaloniki and president of the 'YOGA ACADEMY NIKOLAOS
MARGIORIS – OMAKOIO') up to this day (December
2010). They draw elements from the work of N. Margioris and make specific references to him and his work
in their bibliography.

A BRIEF SUMMARY
OF THE PRESENT WORK

A unique and unprecedented presence in the universal
bibliographical annals, the Free Spiritual Explanation of
the most basic and disputed points of the Apocalypse of
John, is now a Fact, directly accessible to all.

In this English work an important part of the Perfect
transcendental Mystical Experience of Nikolaos A. Margioris (1913-1993), the Master of the Spirit, is revealed for
the first time.

It concerns a modern Greek-orthodox Christocentric
and Christocratic Mystic who sheds ample Light on the
Interpretation of the Apocalypse and who penetrates its
innermost core, touching the Inner Greatness, Depth and
Ecstasy that comes from a true child of the Spirit, John
the Apostle.

With particular care, he removes one by one the veils
of the most deeply symbolized - enigmatic words that
decorate it, presenting the illuminating Unbuilt Light that
directs the future of ALL Omnicreation according to the
Divine Plan.

At the same time, he clearly Separates it from any
earthly - rationalistic and generally untrue interpretations
floating around and places it among the highest Visionary

conceptions of the Spirit that only the Worthy (the proper vessels) are able to touch.

In simple terms (Esotericism for all), with colloquial expressions and full of hyperintellectual Knowledge converted to intellectual meanings, he shows and initiates the seeker in the bottomless depth and the unfathomable height of Divine Expression, of the Laws that rule it and of the beings that live and are evolved within it.

An uncompromising and spiritually integral Cosmogonic and Eschatological approach, an extremely rare hyperconscious document, a deep and substantial addition that will remain monumental in earthly time is described with great detail and analysis, while at the same time it constitutes a safe compass and a solid spiritual point of reference for everyone interested.

The work is accompanied by the extensive analytical commendations of the Master's student, Ilias L. Katsiampas who clarifies what is being explained, while at the same time sounding out our times. He examines and "prescribes" the future, having the present and the position of man in it as a strong criterion, and especially in relation with all the doomsday literature, the prophesying - prophecology and the scaremongering that persecutes us and that disorientates us to a great extent and makes us stray from our real duties and responsibilities. But it also examines how the outer and inner Opening of man when facing the future and especially in relation with the spiritual that is found behind Everything must be attained.

All that can and must be given in our present time is presented to the physical observer by a genuine modern Initiate who walked quietly beside us, producing a titanic body of Spiritual Work (more than 180 metaphysical and practical books) flowing from the Complete Spiritual Experiences he had, which constitute the crowning of Spiritual Power in His worthy Vessel.

A comprehensible and comprehensive piece of Work that is a reference point in the spiritual happenings of our country and through which the true continuation of the Perfect Mystical conception and the conveyance of Transcendental Knowledge are secured. With its thorough explanations, it openhandedly and with Ample Love unfolds in front of us the skein of the Whole of Creation.

A Splendid piece of Work that comes from one of the Great Spiritual Children of Greece and that will undoubtedly remain in the spiritual history of our country as unforgettable and beneficial in every way.

A BRIEF SUMMARY
OF THE PRESENT WORK

A different, distinguished, unique in the universal bibliography explanation of the Apocalypse of John through the prism of the Transcendental, Visionary, Mystical Experience of a modern Christocentric and Christocratic Mystic, Nikolaos A. Margioris, the Greek Master.

It is an unprecedented Cosmogonic and Eschatological Conception of the Divine Expression, of the Laws that rule the Beings that live and evolve within it.

An important spiritual interpretation-teaching, given orally by the Master, concise and to-the-point, and that is brought today to the wider public by his student-writer, who with his extensive analytical commendations clears up the matter of prophesying and doomsday scenarios floating around us, always according to the Perfect Mystical Conception of his Master (he wrote and published more than 180 Metaphysical and practical works) and the generally accepted spiritual tradition that comes from all Great persons.

Finally, it defines the evolution of our times and "foretells" the future in relation with the technocratic evolution and mainly with the spiritual evolution that is opening up before us.

A splendid Asset that comes from one of the Great Spiritual Children of Greece and that will undoubtedly remain in the spiritual history of our country as unforgettable and beneficial in every way.

An invaluable Esoteric Gem that must not be omitted from any library.

A more extensive analysis of the work exists in the library.

ISBN 978-960-85735-6-7

www.ingramcontent.com/pod-product-compliance
Lightning Source LLC
LaVergne TN
LVHW041253080426
835510LV00009B/716